Kazakhstan

Kazakhstan

Surprises and Stereotypes
After 20 Years of Independence

JONATHAN AITKEN

continuum

Published by the Continuum International Publishing Group

The Tower Building   80 Maiden Lane
11 York Road   Suite 704
London   New York
SE1 7NX   NY 10038

www. continuumbooks.com

First published 2012

British Library Cataloguing-in-Publication Data
A catalogue record for this book is available from the British Library.

ISBN: HB: 978-1-4411-1654-3

Library of Congress Cataloging-in-Publication Data
A catalog record for this book is available from the Library of Congress.

Typeset by Fakenham Prepress Solutions, Fakenham, Norfolk NR21 8NN
Printed and bound in Great Britain

To Anuar Adilbekov

My twenty-four year old Kazakh Godson whose youthful ambition, fluent English, Bolashak scholarship and dedication to public service symbolizes all that is best in the rising generation of his country.

Contents

Acknowledgements

When I completed my last book, *Nazarbayev and the Making of Kazakhstan* one or two friends suggested that I should consider a sequel. Their idea was that having written the first Western biography of the President I should try to create a portrait of the country.

I was intrigued by the idea for two reasons. First, I find the Kazakhstanis an attractive people who are building a nation that has many more surprising aspects to it than most foreign writing suggests. Secondly, I have become mildly irritated by the out of date stereotypes of Kazakhstan which are repeated too easily in the international media.

So this book is my author's attempt at capturing the new spirit of contemporary Kazakhstan. Inevitably it is a subjective portrait but inspired by so many experiences and individuals that I hope there is plenty of objectivity too! The responsibility for all reporting and commenting is entirely my own. But after interviewing (in the course of both books) over one hundred sources, one or two figures stand out to whom I express special gratitude. The first is President Nursultan Nazarbayev whose willingness to give me over 35 hours of one-on-one interviews has been matched by his openness, his humour and his unique perspectives.

Secondly, I thank Erlan Idrissov, former Foreign Minister of Kazakhstan, former Ambassador in London and now his country's Ambassador in Washington DC. He is an electrifyingly effective bridge builder of understanding between Western minds and Kazakhstani minds. To him and his colleagues at the Ministry of Foreign Affairs I am particularly grateful, not least for the in-country hospitality they arranged for me.

Kazakhstan is a young country increasingly driven by its younger generation. I have talked and enjoyed hospitality with many of them. One became such a good friend that he is now my adopted Kazakh Godson. He is 24 year old Anuar Adilbekov, a Bolashak scholar who has spent much of the past year studying at Essex University in Britain. We first met in Stepnogorsk prison – when he was accompanying me on a tour of Kazakh jails as the representative of his boss Marat Beketayev (another special friend) who is Executive Secretary of the Ministry of Justice. Because Anuar Adilbekov is such a symbolic representative of the talented rising generation of Kazakhstan this book is dedicated to him and to them.

Most of the typing of the book was carried out by Rosemary Gooding with extra help from Helen Kirkpatrick and Susanna Jennens. To all of them my warm thanks. For useful research work I am grateful to Anuar Adilbekor and to my daughter Victoria Aitken

I also thank my publishers, Continuum, particularly Robin Baird-Smith and Rhodri Mogford.

Finally, the greatest gratitude of all goes to my beloved wife Elizabeth who gracefully tolerated my absences from home on visits to Kazakhstan and encouraged me on every step of my authors' journey.

JONATHAN AITKEN
London, July 2011

1
Towards a New National Identity

Towards a New National Identity

Writing about contemporary Kazakhstan is like making a journey into unexplored territory, for it is one of the least known yet most surprising nations of the post Soviet world. It may be a timely moment to offer a portrait of this new country as it passes the historical milestone of its twentieth anniversary as an independent state.

At the time of Kazakhstan's premature birth into independence, conceived amidst the chaos of the Soviet Union's disintegration in December 1991, the consensus of opinion held that the infant nation was too poor and too politically unstable to survive. This view, later encouraged by ridicule from the movie *Borat,* prevailed for several years.

Today the international community takes Kazakhstan seriously because of its growing economic importance. Yet even now most westerners know little or nothing about its history, culture, character and future potential. Nevertheless there is a growing understanding that a new powerhouse is coming of age on the Steppes. At this strategic crossroads where Chinese, Russian, Central Asian and Western civilizations converge, Kazakhstan has arrived as a stable and significant nation state.

One sign of the changing times is that international recognition of Kazakhstan is rising. From its hosting of the OSCE summit to the performances of its acclaimed orchestras and musicians, the country is making its mark on the world stage. Its economic power to move oil markets, stock markets, grain markets and the world uranium market is well known to global traders. Kazakhstanis themselves are becoming more confident as they travel and study abroad in large numbers. This is a nation on the move.

Kazakhstan's governance and politics are interesting too, although you would never guess it from the lazy reporting of too much of the world's media. Stereotypes and clichés abound, among them 'police state'; 'ruthless dictatorship'; 'sinister regime'; and even 'worse than North Korea'. Forgive them their press passes! This author has been able to report from the country's darkest corners, such as its prisons and security services; on its brightest scholars and students; on its cultural show pieces of theatre, ballet and music; from its rural *auls*; its intellectual schools; its richest industries; its liveliest young entrepreneurs; its two greatest cities and in interviews with its most prominent public figures. At the end of such a writer's journey I have no complaints about lack of access or openness. As a result, this book contains some criticisms, some compliments, and many fresh insights. The most intriguing discovery is the emergence of a new national identity.

Portraying the national identity at the time of Kazakhstan's twentieth anniversary is challenging because the picture is not static. So much in the country is developing and changing fast. Yet for all its growing wealth, the nation's most important resource is its people. They are a combination of the talented and the traditional, full of futuristic ambition yet with deep roots in their ancestry and culture. Defining these roots is difficult because they are a fusion of ancient Steppe values; Turkic-Islamic heritage; and the testing experiences of Soviet colonisation. To understand Kazakhstan's past and potential, three themes are surprisingly important: Suffering, Survival and Success.

National character can be strengthened in adversity. By this measure the resilience of the Kazakhstani people was tested to the full by the tragic sagas of their twentieth century sufferings.

The first of these tragedies was the Bolshevik revolution of 1917. Uprooted from their ancestral lands by the revolutionary ending of the Russian empire, 1.5 million Kazakh nomads fled with their herds of sheep and cattle into China and Mongolia in the early 1920s.

The second tragedy was the Communist policy of agricultural collectivizm which had a devastating effect on the remaining nomads and their livestock. Between 1930 and 1933 over three million Kazakhstanis died of starvation as they were forced off their traditional pastures and into the disastrous experiment of Soviet-directed collective farms.

Accompanying collectivism came the reign of terror and repression ordered by Josef Stalin. He subjugated the Kazakhs with ruthless brutality. At least 300,000 of them were executed or died between 1937–54. These losses were accompanied by deportations into Kazakhstan of 500,000 victims of Stalin's purges from other parts of the Soviet Union.

Many of these deportees were prisoners incarcerated in a network of sinister penal camps – *The Gulag*. An extra dimension to the sorrows of twentieth century Kazakhstan was added by the realisation that its northern territory became the principal location, after Siberia, for these prisons.

Whether they were locked up in the *Gulag* or dumped into collective farms, this compulsory migration of multi-ethnic foreigners diluted the indigenous Kazakh people still further. In addition to Stalin's deportees, when Nikita Khrushchev ruled the Soviet Union over a million workers were moved to another disastrous agricultural experiment on Kazakh soil – the Virgin Lands Scheme. By this time the Kazakhs had become an oppressed minority in their own country, almost losing their way of life. Reduced to a rump of 37 per cent of the population their nationhood was steadily suppressed by their Soviet occupiers – for example, by 1961 the capital city of Almaty was allowed only one Kazakh language high school.

Perhaps the most terrifying exploitation of Kazakhstan during the Soviet era was the use of the Semipalatinsk region as a nuclear weapons testing site. Between 1949 and 1989 tests took place there at the rate of one every three weeks. In those four decades there were 752 nuclear explosions in Kazakhstan – 114 of them in the atmosphere or at ground level with no protection for the domestic population. The regularity and radioactivity of these tests had appalling consequences for the national environment and for the health of the local people. As a result, a climate of fear and revulsion spread across the Soviet Republic of Kazakhstan when the secrets of Moscow's nuclear testing program began to leak out through deformed births, increased cancer rates, crops disease and other horrors. The mental and physical scars of these radiation effects are still felt deep in the heart of Kazakh society today.

Understanding the ordeals of the country's twentieth century past provides a clearer perspective of its twenty-first century future. For Kazakhstanis are tough, stoical people well schooled in surviving the climatic extremes of the steppes and the political extremism of colonial occupiers. Despite many efforts to obliterate them, Kazakhstan's language, poetry, music and national character were well preserved in times of suffering and are now flourishing in times of success.

This spirit of survival was needed after the Soviets departed in 1991. Independence in the ruins of the collapsed super power was initially more painful than joyful. The country was left bankrupt and dysfunctional. It had no currency, rampant inflation, inadequate food production and useless factories. Pensions and salaries could not be paid by the government. Families went hungry. The country teetered on the brink of economic and political chaos. But during the first few years of self government its people discovered moral as well as material assets which enabled them to pull though the many crises they had to endure.

The first of these moral assets was tolerance. Kazakhstan is a country made up of over 138 nationalities and ethnic groups. The parents and grandparents of today's society were thrown together in adversity. The rising generation of their descendants have learned to live together in prosperity. This national chemistry of flexibility and tolerance is a miraculous successor to the previous era of oppression. Kazakhstan has become the melting pot of Asia as its sorrows fade into memories. It is a young country whose 16 million people have an average age of 31. Their eyes are fixed optimistically on the future with a second moral quality underpinning their tolerance. It is their trust – in each other and their leadership.

Building a new country is exhilarating as it becomes successful. Trust grows as results are achieved. Twenty years ago Kazakhstan was an impoverished and backward Central Asian state. Today it is the power-house of the region, rising in economic performance and international respect.

Since independence Kazakhstan's GDP per capita has risen twelvefold and exceeds $9,000 – a level of prosperity roughly equivalent to

Malaysia's. It is climbing so much faster than in most other emerging economies that the GDP per capita figure is forecast to reach $28,000 by 2020.

The current rate of unemployment, now 5.6 per cent, is falling and is lower than in the United States, Britain, France and Germany. Perhaps the most hopeful sign of all is the arrival of a young and ambitious middle class. Too many of them seem to prefer a safe career in government to an entrepreneurial career in business but that also is changing.

Economic statistics tell only one part of the story. As the title of this book suggests, Kazakhstan is full of surprises. Its people are warm, hospitable, good humoured, open-minded, cultured, fond of telling stories, frequently musical, splendidly convivial and full of laughter and *joie de vivre*. They are an attractive nationality whose qualities range from physical beauty to Steppes-centred romanticism.

Inevitably, an ex-Soviet country has its faults and failings. Although Kazakhstan feels like a free society it has not yet become one. The Soviet legacy dies hard in many of the national institutions. Parliament is comprised of only one party. The courts and judiciary are not delivering well because of the lack of new judges with high standards. There is too much corruption. The media is restricted. A fully fledged democracy with truly free and fair elections is some way off. However, as later chapters of this book show there are signs of real progress in most of these areas.

Western democracies have a tendency to be cynical and mistrustful towards political leaders. Kazakhstani public opinion takes the opposite tack. This is partly because of traditional respect for seniority and hierarchy and partly because the people genuinely trust their President. They look on him as the founding father of their nation and refer to him, affectionately, as *Papa*.

The trust and the affection have grown because President Nursultan Nazarbayev has delivered. Kazakhstan, at its present level of development, would not have survived without his leadership through the years of turbulence. My previous book *Nazarbayev and the Making of Kazakhstan* (Continuum 2009) tells his story. Yet even since this biography was written the country has leapt out of recession and into international prominence. These achievements were made possible by a rising tide of confidence at all levels.

This book tries to analyse the spirit and identity of the country as it reaches the twentieth anniversary of its independence. A good starting point for this analysis is the surprisingly creative tension between New Kazakhstan and Old Kazakhstan.

2

New Kazakhstan
v
Old Kazakhstan

(I) THE SURPRISE OF THE NON-REFERENDUM

In the early weeks of 2011 there was a power struggle between New Kazakhstan and Old Kazakhstan. New Kazakhstan won.

Since most of the arguments in this discreet dispute took place well below the parapet of public debate few people could understand what was happening, let alone appreciate the significance of what eventually emerged. But now it is possible to lift the veil and relate the story as a fascinating chapter in Kazakhstan's political development. This episode gives many clues to the future direction of the country as it reaches the twentieth anniversary of its independence.

At the end of 2010, Kazakhstan and its President were on the crest of a wave. The country had weathered the storms of international recession in far better shape than most experts predicted. Although the 2008-9 global banking crisis had hit the construction companies and the financial sector, the slump struck early, the right measures were applied, so recovery came more swiftly and strongly than in the US and Europe. By the autumn of what was expected to be a difficult year, Kazakhstan's economic growth had climbed to 7 per cent, unemployment was down to 5 per cent and the government felt able to announce a number of confidence building measures such as a 25 per cent pay rise for public service employees and several major infrastructure projects.

The most important boost to national self confidence was a diplomatic success: the holding of the OSCE summit in Astana on December 1–2 2010. To outside observers it may seem strange that a conference under the leadership of an international organization whose initials many people would have difficulty recognising (OSCE = Organization for Security and Cooperation in Europe) could cause a surge of political excitement in the host country. Yet as detailed in Chapter 9 of this book, this is precisely what happened. When 56 national leaders flew into Astana for the summit (headed by US Secretary of State Hillary Clinton; President Dmitri Medvedev of Russia; Chancellor Angela Merkel of Germany; President Nicolas Sarkozy of France and Prime

Minister Silvio Berlusconi of Italy) Kazakhstanis at all levels in society felt immense pride at their country's arrival on the world stage as a respected and recognized player.

In the aftermath of the OSCE summit there was an understandable sense of elation among Kazakhstan's political elite. Most of them were men over 50 or older who grew up in the former Soviet Union, were educated in Soviet Universities and who are still imbued, however hard they may try to break away from it, with a Soviet mentality. It is no disrespect to describe this group as 'Old Kazakhstan'. They are still the backbone of the government, which despite occasional mistakes and failings, they have served well.

Old Kazakhstan likes the status quo, which to them means their jobs under the present system of Presidential patronage. So in the warm glow of mutual admiration following the OSCE summit they came up with a method of praising their President and preserving their own position. This was described as 'The Referendum to extend the President's term in office'.

Their political initiative started mysteriously in the eastern city of Ust-Kamenogorsk when a forum of 850 provincial citizens voted unanimously to exercise their constitutional right to demand a referendum. Its objective was to cancel the presidential election scheduled for the end of 2012 and to extend President Nazarbayev's term in office to 2020. The leader of this 'citizen's initiative' was an obscure University Rector Erlan Sydykov, but he was evidently being backed by far more heavyweight political figures. For within ten days of the forum, the referendum had been registered by the Central Election Commission, authorized by a vote in Parliament and supported by 300,000 signatories, 100,000 more than the number required to call a referendum under the constitution. Two weeks later the number of signatories had grown to 5 million, although it also became clear from critical comments posted anonymously on the internet that a significant number of students, teachers, business people and government officials were complaining of being put under pressure to sign the petition.

President Nazarbayev professed surprise at the referendum initiative and handled it by referring the matter to the Constitutional Council. However this was a delaying mechanism rather than an outright rejection. It seemed extremely unlikely that such a proposal would ever have got so far without some form of tacit presidential approval. The explanation doing the rounds was that leading figures from Old Kazakhstan had 'bounced' the referendum on Nazarbayev. He was initially attracted by it, reinforced in his attraction by the more traditional expressions of support from the rural areas, yet his sixth sense of political caution told him to handle it with care.

Other voices were urging him to kill the referendum stone dead. The western diplomatic community was horrified that on the coat-tails of an OSCE summit designed to strengthen democracy the host country should be contemplating such an anti-democratic move. But envoys have no votes and their views were not being forcefully expressed at face to face presidential meetings, particularly as there was no US Ambassador in post. From Almaty, traditionally the most liberal city, senior figures in the business community seemed to like the idea of the stability that ten more years of undisturbed Nazarbayev power would produce. So it was left to the younger generation of internet bloggers to denounce the referendum proposal as an 'old style Communist conjuring trick'. Their protest did not appear to be cutting much ice.

Nazarbayev is a wily political operator. He listens carefully to all sources of advice and engages in both sides of a debate. So when speaking to friends who visited him in his Akorda office in the last week of January 2011 he started to present the arguments in favour of the referendum. He began by explaining the ancient traditions of 'steppes democracy' by which the Khans listened to their subjects and then ruled in accordance with the people's will. 'People are telling me that this referendum movement is a return to our historic rules', he explained. 'So at first I joked about it saying, 'How can we possibly go back to the ways this country was governed 1,500 years ago?'

'But now I have had to recognize the facts and figures. Five and a half million people have signed the referendum to extend my term.

They represent 70 to 75 per cent of the people who are eligible to vote in any election. In effect they are voting for me now. I don't need this referendum myself. I am confident that I will be re-elected at the next presidential election in 2012. So I haven't engineered this referendum demand in order to be criticized. Yet I can't just ignore it. The situation is like what has been happening in Tunisia and Egypt only the other way round. There the people were demanding that their leader should go. Here they are demanding that I should stay! And I can't just disregard the wishes of 5.5 million people. Yet I am a little uncomfortable about it and I feel I am in a delicate situation, particularly now that Parliament has voted for the referendum too'.

Nazarbayev then ran over the pressures on him and the options available to him. He made the point that the referendum enthusiasts had put him into a position that was 'impeccable' under the constitution. But he was holding back. Western opinion was a factor, but not a decisive one. Much more important were the views of the country and doing what was right for his people. As he went over the old ground of not rejecting the demands of more than 5 million voters, his uncertainty was puzzling against a background of such certainty served up by the referendum campaigners.

As his summary of internal debate went backwards and forwards it became clear that Nazarbayev had not yet made up his own mind. Using friends as a sounding board he was still thinking aloud, weighing the pro-referendum advice from his own inner circle with the conflicting views coming in from an outer circle on such matters as legacy issues, diplomatic pressures and the mood among the younger generation. It was fascinating to see the President's decision making process swinging in one direction and then in another. But his paramount concern was for the good governance of Kazakhstan as he eventually said:

'We are developing a democratic system here and I don't want to give the wrong signal to the next generation of politicians', he said. 'I don't want them to think that elections are not competitive'. He again re-iterated his personal confidence in being re-elected at the scheduled date for the next presidential election in 2012 or of being re-appointed for an extended term by re-election. So the issue was not about him.

'But there might be a third option', mused the President. 'I could say that as a response to the millions of people who are wanting a referendum I will instead call an early election in 2011. Anyone could stand against me. It would be an open and constitutional election.'

By the end of a long conversation, it seemed as though the President was tilting towards the early election option. But although he sounded convinced he stayed cautious. His position was that he needed more time before he could make a final decision.

Time was running out because at the end of January the political calendar of Kazakhstan was marked for an important event – the annual State of the Nation address by the President to the upper and lower houses of Parliament. Clearly modelled on the State of the Union speech by the President of the United States to Congress, this 2011 address was creating a strong buzz of advance interest since Nazarbayev was thought likely to announce that the referendum to extend his term would be going ahead.

The assembled audience of 107 Members of the Majilis, 47 Senators and about 60 Ministers and Vice Ministers all looked expectant as the President began his State of the Nation speech. Most of it was a predictable and well practised recital of Kazakhstan's achievements since independence. The air was soon thick with detailed statistics about growth rates, schools, hospitals, job creation, agricultural production, pension increases and foreign policy achievements. It was familiar material to most of those present, so familiar to one elderly Senator that he fell asleep. But everyone woke up when the President came to the penultimate passage of his address.

'Dear people of Kazakhstan', he began in a tone suggesting that a momentous announcement was imminent. 'You all know about the initiative of holding the referendum to extend the term of office of the head of state?' Many members of the audience shifted forwards on their seats in rapt attention.

But to general amazement, the conclusion of the State of the Nation speech had no conclusion. It was as if Beethoven had composed a symphony without a last movement. Instead of the expected *allegro vivace* crescendo of ringing chords, clashing cymbals and the full orchestra at *fortissimo* there was the oratorical equivalent of an anti-climatic *dimuendo* amounting to … well … er … um … not much to say on this really.

Far from giving a clear message on the referendum issue that was gripping the county, Nazarbayev rolled out a few final bromides such as 'Love for the motherland means one has to meet all challenges it sends' and 'If the country has a blessing its direction will be right'. American politicians would have called this a 'motherhood and apple pie' ending. The ancient Greeks might have said 'The Oracle at Delphi has spoken but we are unable to interpret the meaning'. The twenty-first century Kazakhstanis were left bemused by the President's indecision.

Nazarbayev was biding his time. He spent the next 48 hours taking the pulse of the nation with the help of the best analysts of public opinion in his Presidential court. Perhaps to his own surprise he found that the silent minority of thoughtful younger citizens were expressing uneasiness about the referendum. This contrasted with view of the more vocal majority of older generation supporters who had already signed up to it. Taking into account the international perspective Nazarbayev came to the clear judgement that the third option of calling an immediate election would be the right decision for the country. So in a surprise national broadcast, he announced that a Presidential election would be held on 3 April.

Although the result of this snap election was never likely to be in doubt the holding of it represented a victory for New Kazakhstan over Old Kazakhstan. A referendum extending the presidential term limit would have been a throwback to the age of Soviet political manipulation. It was designed to delight the old guard but it would have left the rising generation dis-satisfied. Their unease would have intensified in the spotlight of international criticism. So Nazarbayev made a good call.

The calls about the arrangements for the election were good too. Although the phrase 'a level playing field' is inappropriate for the electoral terrain of a country whose politics are dominated by a founding father equivalent to George Washington, there was equality of opportunity in the rules for candidates. Anyone could run for the Presidency who was able to collect the required 90,000 signatures on their nomination papers and pass a simple Kazakh language test. These were not serious obstacles for any serious candidate and the three who qualified themselves to enter the contest each received a state funding grant of 6.8 million KZT (approximately US$50,000) and the promise of fair coverage in the state media. How the election worked out in terms of its freedom and fairness is analysed in later sections of this chapter. But the initial decision to reject the referendum and to go to the polls on 3 April was right. New Kazakhstan was pleased by it.

* * *

(II) ELECTION DAY AND THE REACTIONS TO THE RESULT

Kazakhstan went to the polls in the Presidential election of 2011 on 3 April. During the voting hours of 7 a.m. to 8 p.m. the weather changed from a sparkling start with azure skies and bright sunshine to a cloudy windswept evening chilled by sleet and snowflakes.

The electoral climate seemed more constant. I visited four of the 218 polling stations in Astana. Voting was steady at all of them. A more unexpected surprise was the mood of the electorate – a combination of the dutiful and the cheerful, occasionally even the joyful.

In the dutiful category came the older residents of Astana, some on sticks or on the arms of friends, all heavily muffled and coated against the minus 4 degree temperature. They had an air of serious determination to go about their business which the Central Electoral Commission's posters outside every polling station proclaimed to be 'Your most important responsibility'.

As a former politician who stood as a candidate in seven UK parliamentary elections between 1974 and 1997, I have an eye for competently and incompetently run polling stations. At the four I visited during the morning and evening events of 3 April in Astana the visible electoral processes could not be seriously faulted. I saw quiet, orderly queuing; simple identification procedures for the issuing of ballots; ballot papers clearly listing the candidates in alphabetical order and private screened off cubicles in which to vote.

The traditional paper method of voting by making a tick or cross against the name of the preferred candidate is the only one now used in Kazakhstan. At previous elections approximately 5 to 7 per cent of the votes had been cast through electronic voting machines. However their unfamiliarity to the electorate and some criticism of the e-system by international observers led to the Electoral Commission's decision to revert in 2011 to the simplest known process.

International observers were present at every polling station I visited. The observers were drawn from a variety of sources. 350 of them were appointed by the OSCE, 420 by the Commonwealth of Independent States, 60 by the Council of Europe and a further 400 came from national parliaments or Non Governmental Organisations (NGOs) around the world. All the observers to whom I spoke said they were satisfied with the voting arrangements on polling day. However one added the rider, 'but we don't know what we don't see'.

Most of the polling stations were located in schools, each one catering for between 1,500 and 3,000 voters in its neighbourhood. A noticeable feature was the youth of the electorate. Astana is a young people's city so most of the voters seemed to be in their mid-20s, which was no great surprise as the average age of the population throughout the country is 31. Many of them brought their families to the polls, often allowing a child to post their completed ballot papers into the box. This family participation created a pleasant atmosphere with many humorous comments such as and 'we are starting the democratic tradition early in our family!' The process looked enjoyable with smiles and positive body language all around. There was little of the dour solemnity that was said to characterize Soviet elections.

At one polling station south of the river, Orbita, some of the voters appeared to have gone into orbit with their joyful celebrations. As I approached I heard rhythmic handclapping, accordion playing at maximum volume and loud cheering. A folk dance session was in full swing at the entrance hall led by pretty young girls in traditional costumes. Apparently the school where the poll was being held had decided to liven up election day by putting on an entertainment by its pupils. Apart from making the queues for the voting booths longer, the carnival atmosphere detracted nothing from the democratic process and added the spirit of good fun. But there were some reservations.

'I wonder if the International Observers will criticize this concert as an election violation?' muttered a diplomat from the French Embassy. A few moments later I found the senior International Observer present at the polling and asked him for his official observations. He was a large rotund gentleman from Tbilisi, Georgia, 'My first observation is that the voting is going smoothly', he said in appropriately serious tone. Then his face creased in smiles as he added, 'And my second observation is that the singer has very pretty legs'.

Youthful legs were also on display at the formal declaration of the count the next day. This event, attended by some 5,000 Astanans, took place on 4 April in the National Sports Centre under the title 'Announcement of the provisional election result'. The proceedings bore a close resemblance to a victory rally at the end of a US Presidential Election. Carefully choreographed for television, the preliminaries contained much oompah and hooplah – dancing girls, rock music, dombra players, folk singers and wave upon wave of cheering. 'Nur-Sultan-Kaz-akh-Stan' was one favourite chant. Another was the Kazakh language equivalent of 'We have won'.

On the dot of twelve noon the noise rose to orgasmic levels of excitement as President Nazarbayev entered the arena flanked by his wife Sarah, his daughter Dariga and her two teenage sons. They made an almost royal procession to the stage while the surging supporters waved aloft their yellow silk scarves bearing the slogan *Moving ahead with our leader*.

The leader himself looked elated but tired as the Deputy Chairman of the Nur Otan Party declared that on the basis of the figures announced by the Central Election Commission, the incumbent President had won

95.5 per cent of the votes cast. The crowd made a passable imitation of surprise at this news and cheered wildly. President Nazarbayev delivered a victory speech full of the post-election sentiments that roll from the lips of politicians all over the world in their hour of triumph:

'This is a victory for all of us ... we have won this together ... we are united as a nation'. He observed that his margin of victory 'might seem sensational in Western eyes'. It was not a qualification that bothered anyone in the Sports Arena that afternoon.

Although the front rows of the hall were well filled by dignitaries from the cabinet and the wider ranks of government, at least three quarters of the victory rally audience were students. Nazarbayev's speech came alive when he directly addressed them. 'You are the future of the country ... students who work hard deserve good jobs, a good life, and a good future'. The words may seem ordinary in print but this *bolashak* (future) passage in the President's remarks evoked an extraordinary response from the galleries of students around the arena. It was a reminder, if one was needed, that Kazakhstan is a young and hopeful country.

Later that afternoon I watched Nazarbayev handle a variety of questions from a press conference for the domestic and international media. None of them raised the point I tackled in my one on one interview with him the following day. Did he have any concern that a 95.5 per cent majority might look so overwhelming to western eyes that there would be suspicions of ballot rigging? 'You have to understand the mentality of a country which is still celebrating the gaining of its independence', replied the President. 'Most of our citizens feel they are seeing Kazakhstan's dream come true. For the first time in their lives they are able to say proudly "I am from Kazakhstan". They reflect this pride in their votes. Also they look around the region they see fifteen states all of them coming into existence when the Soviet Union collapsed and all of them starting with similar prospects. Kazakhstan has done much better than any of them economically. "Our GDP is three times larger than our nearest competitor Ukraine. So we have really good results for our citizens to vote for" '.

Nazarbayev is entitled to make these claims from his own proud viewpoint as 'Father of the Nation' (an official title bestowed on him by a parliamentary vote in 2009). He is genuinely popular with the electorate and the level of support for him is high. But is it credible that his successes should have earned him a 95.5 per cent majority?One group of people who were unconvinced were the 350 observers supplied by the OSCE. Their post election report noted 'serious irregularities including numerous instances of seemingly identical signatures on voter lists and cases of ballot box stuffing. The vote count and tabulation of results lacked transparency'.

Other teams of international observers were more generous. The Parliamentary Assembly of the Council of Europe said in their statement, 'Despite certain imperfections that inevitably mar all elections in any country the outcome of this vote truly reflects the will of the electorate'. The Independent International Observer Mission assessed the election as successful on three levels. 'First, it clearly reflects the political choice of Kazakhstan's voters', said the IOM statement, 'Second, it marks a definite advance in the transparency of the electoral process compared with previous elections. And third, it opens the prospect for the formation of a more pluralist or multiparty Parliament in the next legislative elections'.

After reading the various groups of international observers reports, talking to several of the individual observers off the record and being on the spot in Astana for election day myself, I felt that Kazakhstan's fledgling democracy deserved at least two and a half cheers.

As all parties agreed, the result was right. The President's landslide reflected the will of the people. The critics may be justified in their allegations that the count was flawed by ballot box stuffing in some districts. Perhaps no-one wanted to be the regional or local Akim whose district scored poorly in the turnout figures or in the recorded size of Nazarbayev's majority. In this context it seemed authentic that the two largest and most sophisticated cities, Astana and Almaty, produced turnouts of around 50 per cent but suspicious that many rural areas had turnouts above 95 per cent.

Although the concerns about vote-inflation had some validity, other criticisms expressed about the election day procedures did not appear to stand up. Most observers praised the atmosphere at the polls for being calm and orderly. One prominent scrutineer Ambassador Daan Everts of the OSCE said he received many reports of voter intimidation and pressure to vote. Other watchers of the election, including this author, felt that the general and sometimes enthusiastic willingness to go to the polls was genuine. Personally I found the positive spirit of the younger electors queuing to vote in and around the polling stations of Astana a moving sign of the national will. In my judgement the big picture showed that a democratic tradition is being built in Kazakhstan, even if in the frame of the 2011 election there remained flaws and irregularities which will need to be corrected in future.

A fair comment made about this presidential election was that it was not sufficiently competitive. True, yet it is not easy to blame anyone for this truth. For historical and political reasons, Nazarbayev towered over the electoral landscape like a giant oak tree. Small acorns and saplings have found it difficult to grow in his shadow but not because he obstructs them. The independent observers' reports showed that the rival candidates were 'by and large given equal coverage' in the news media, and provided with state finance for their campaigns. There were some complaints about the lack of analytical election programs on television and some grievances about the blocking of websites run by the independent newspaper *Respublica* and the TV channel *K+*. But even if these concerns were justified they had only a peripheral impact on the course of the election campaign and virtually no impact at all on the result.

So Nazarbayev deserved his victory. It was a fair and legitimate verdict of the people, even though some of the election procedures were not fully democratic in terms of vote counting and candidate competiveness.

Although the overwhelming majority of Kazakhstanis accepted the result and were glad to see President Nazarbayev in power for another five year term, the political restlessness which surfaced over the referendum issue has not gone away. The tensions between Old Kazakhstan and New Kazakhstan are still on the agenda. Who will seek to make progress with the reform program of that agenda? To understand both the obstacles and the opportunities that could lie ahead it is necessary to begin with a look at the opposition.

*   *   *

(III) DOES THE OPPOSITION EXIST?

Making sense of Kazakhstan's opposition is difficult, largely because its parties make so little sense themselves. To describe them as weak, fragmented and contradictory is to understate their problems, many of which are self-created. However the very concept of opposition is poorly understood in a state which has not yet reformed its political system away from the Soviet model. So this part of Kazakhstani politics is only at the early stages of work in progress.

On the internet, anyone can describe themselves as 'an opposition leader' and many do. At the time of the referendum proposal at least six individuals claiming to represent a political party issued statements attacking the plan to extend the President's term until 2020. These organizations had names like the *Algha* or Forward Party; and the Long Live Liberty group. However, when I made efforts to get in touch with them it appeared they were one man bands existing only in cyberspace with no tangible administrative or support base.

The nearest approximation to a credible opposition party is ANSDP-AZAT (All National Social Democratic Party) whose co-chairmen I met in Almaty in January 2011. They were Bulat Abilov an energetic 53 year old businessman whose resources largely finance ANSDP-AZAT and Jarmahan Tuyakbayev a former Prosecutor General and an ex-Deputy Leader of the President Nur Otan Party. Both had become disenchanted with the government on account of its failure to develop democratic reforms or to allow free, fair and competitive elections.

Bulat Abilov voiced a catalogue of other political criticisms which included demands to create an independent court system; to decentralize power away from the presidency; to fight corruption more effectively; and to ensure that the wealth of the country should be shared more widely. He developed this agenda in our interview with a passion which resembled the quick fire delivery of Neil Kinnock on speed. Abilov declared (and his co-chair Tuyakbayev assented) that he would be their party's candidate in the next presidential election. Although he did not expect to beat the incumbent Nazarbayev, he said he was confident of getting enough votes to put down a marker for the future which would enable him to be a serious competitor in any democratic election for the succession.

Having filled many pages of notes as I recorded Bulat Abilov's opinions I came away from my interview with certainty that he intended to run for the presidency. So it astonished me and most other observers of the political scene when neither Abilov nor Tuyakbayev nor the ANSDP-AZAT party contested the 2011 Presidential election. There was no coherent explanation for their withdrawal from the race as their opponents were quick to point out.

'They made complete fools of themselves', said Senator Gani Kassymov who stood on behalf of the rival Patriotic Party against Nazarbayev. 'They held a conference to announce their strategy for the Presidential Election. At the end of the morning session it was unanimously decided that the ANDSP-AZAT party had chosen Bulat Abilov to be their candidate. Then they had a lunch break and in the afternoon they decided they were going to boycott the whole election. They must have been trying to get into the Guinness Book of Records for the weirdest and fastest U-Turn!'

This ridicule is justified. The cosmetic excuse for the contortions of ANSDP-AZAT was that they felt the sudden calling of an election did not give them enough time to prepare their campaign. This was not a convincing stance from a leadership which opposed the referendum and wanted a presidential contest at the polls. An alternative and more likely explanation is that there were feuds and personality clashes within the party. Whatever the reason, the disappointing result was that the largest and most experienced opposition group decided to stay on the sidelines of the 2011 election.

The absence of ANSDP-AZAT meant that the President faced weak opposition in the shape of three candidates who had little or no organization behind them. The Communist Party's choice, Zhambyl Akhmetbekov, predictably demanded the nationalisation of all major businesses and a radical re-distribution of wealth. The Green Party's leader, Mels Yeleussizov, spoke up for the environment and the rural areas. Neither made much impact, each receiving around one per cent of the poll.

The runner up in the election, Senator Gani Kassymov, won almost twice as many votes (1.9 per cent) but made more impression on the electorate. This was partly because he is a better known and more engaging public figure. He has a nice line in self deprecating humour and an unavoidable *basso profundo* voice, as loud as a ship's foghorn.

More significantly, Kassymov produced a serious eight page election manifesto calling for political and constitutional reforms. The main issues on which he campaigned included re-establishing the office of vice-president; giving more power to Parliament; expanding the rights of political parties; and reforming the judicial and law enforcement agencies of the state so that they would become independent of the executive. Interviewing him two days after the election result I asked him why such an apparently sensible program should have received so few votes.

'Actually I did rather well! I came second and I received over 160,000 votes which is not at all bad for a moth-eaten old blanket like me', boomed Kassymov, 'and I have no doubt that my ideas will take root. There is an old saying on the steppes "a struggle for the throne provides the opportunity to do good things for society which have not been done before". That is exactly what has happened as a result of my campaign. If you look carefully at the small print of what the President said in his speeches immediately after the election you will see that he has already started to borrow my ideas. He has stopped talking the usual nonsense about how we must put economics first and then move slowly towards political reform. One day after the election he began starting to talk about reforming parliament and other institutions'.

Whether or not Senator Gani Kassymov deserves the credit for it, there is truth in the observation that Nazarbayev did move swiftly after the election to pick out some of the better ideas from his opponents platforms and announce them as part of his own program for the future direction of the country. This approach is analysed in the final section of this chapter: *Signposts for the Future.*

Whatever he thought of their policies, the weakness of the opposition's parties and personalities were criticized by the President when I interviewed him two days after his election victory.

'Unfortunately they are led mainly by civil servants who failed, that is why not many people listen to them', he said 'but they should build their support in the local government assemblies. That is the arena where they should test their skills and show what they are made of'.

Asked about the future national Parliamentary elections, Nazarbayev seemed ambivalent about whether any reforms were needed. In the last election of 2007, the President's party Nur Otan won every single seat in the 107 seat Majilis or lower house. This was because the rules of the proportional representation system laid down in the constitution created a threshold figure of seven per cent that had to be reached before a party could begin to win seats in the Majilis. In 2007 the only two opposition parties to trouble the scorers ANSDP and Ak Zohl took respectively 4.6 per cent and 3.3 per cent of the votes cast so failed to be represented in parliament. Seen with the wisdom of hindsight it was probably an embarrassment that the rules ended up creating a one-party lower house. Nazarbayev now says that consideration is being given to bringing forward a constitutional amendment that will lower the threshold figure for Majilis seats from seven per cent to five or four per cent. This would give a fillip to the growth of opposition representation in parliament but no decision on this constitutional change has yet been taken.

Another route for developing the concept of opposition in parliamentary debate is to encourage coalition politics. 'Maybe Nur Otan should split off a wing, or maybe more opposition parties should unite together instead of fragmenting', says Nazarbayev with a vagueness which implies that this is not a subject that comes high on his agenda.

In fact there are some stirrings in this direction. One of the most articulate opposition politicians is Alikhan Baimenov who chairs the Ak Zhol party. He is a former automobile industry engineer and senior government executive who headed Kazakhstan's Civil Service Agency. He turned to politics during a stormy period of upheavals which culminated in the murder of a leading opposition figure Altynbek Sarsenbayev in 2006. Contrary to later rumours spread by the President's disaffected son-in-law Rakhat Aliyev from his exile in Vienna, Nazarbayev was not involved in this crime nor was his chief of staff. However, the Sarsenbayev tragedy was an important factor in stunting the advancement of opposition politics in Kazakhstan. For it created a climate of fear and repression which has not entirely evaporated even though critics of the government are now increasingly free to voice their complaints and to form opposition parties.

Alikhan Baimenov has passed through his period of antagonism towards the monolithic state of his country's politics. He says that he and the Ak Zohl party he leads are now taking the road of 'constructive opposition'. He believes that this means co-operating with the President's party in a future parliament in order to change the way people think about politics. Ak Zohl's motto is a quotation from the poet Abay 'Only the blind do not see the achievements; only the ignorant do not see the faults'.

In the spirit of Abay, Alikhan Baimenov is generous about Nazarbayev's achievements, giving particular praise to the economic growth of the country and to the international recognition gained through the OSCE. 'It really was extraordinary how the conference captivated our nation. Even at wedding parties we found ourselves drinking toasts to the bride, the groom *and* the OSCE. Little babies born at this time were named 'Summit' or 'Summita', he says, 'you have to admire Nazarbayev for succeeding in this effort of nation building and bringing us into such international prominence'.

On the other hand Baimenov favours major policy changes on the domestic front. He wants to move the country away from its Russian roots by abolishing the Cyrillic alphabet from the Kazakh language and replacing it with the Latin script. He believes that the rising number of young people attending mosques is sending a signal that spiritual values are important to politics. 'We don't want any forms of radical Islam here but we do need a recognition that there is more to life than materialism', says Baimenov, who is himself the son of a Sunni spiritual leader.

In promoting this emphasis on new values, Ak Zohl is committed to parliamentary reforms that will result in making the executive of ministers more accountable to the legislature and expanding the rights of voters. Baimenov wants to see half the members of the Majilis directly elected by local constituencies and half winning their seats through the party list system. He believes that the President's personal popularity is real and quite different from the popularity of the Nur Otan Party which has a much lower level of support. 'I keep in touch with the ordinary people in the streets and in the auls (villages) and I would estimate that somewhere between 25 per cent and 40 per cent of the electorate would like to vote for another party with a program of change – provided this does not cause instability. So this is what my party is voting towards – change with stability. And I believe our greatest ally in bringing this about is likely to be President Nazarbayev because he clearly understands that political reforms are necessary'.

It is a strange aspect of Kazakhstani politics that the opposition leaders are waiting for the incumbent president to put forward proposals for political reform. This is not just because the opposition parties are fragmented. It is also because Kazakh traditionalism runs deep. According to that tradition the leader (once the Khan now the President) is so revered for his seniority and wisdom that open criticism of him is considered bad form. This seems extraordinary in western eyes where political traditions are full of irreverence to the point of aggressive polarisation. But it is not the Kazakh way of politics.

The 2011 presidential election was notable for its lack of personal attacks between the candidates or even in the columns of opposition newspapers like *Respublica*. Cynics will say this is because free speech is partially suppressed and robust political debate is discouraged. Optimists argue that an election without rancour yet with genuine differences on future policy being aired is a step forward on the road to democratic progress. The vote count may have been fudged but the reforming tendency made its presence felt. The voices of this tendency spoke in muted murmurs rather than divisive declarations. This is because they are a loyal opposition, respectful of the President personally even while being critical of his government politically. They are mostly too young to remember the Soviet era, getting their higher education outside Kazakhstan, travelling to foreign countries for their vacations, and well tuned to the internet. The views of the rising generation are not yet significantly expressed by voting for the lacklustre list of opposition politicians. However, this generation's opinions can easily be heard in hundreds if not thousands of conversations in cafes, student halls of residence and private homes. This is the New Kazakhstan which is quietly talking. Is Old Kazakhstan listening?

*   *   *

(IV) SIGNPOSTS FOR THE FUTURE

The President is certainly listening and so is his youthful but experienced Prime Minister Karim Massimov who was re-appointed to his post immediately after the election.

Old Kazakhstan, which still thinks that top jobs should be shared out between regional and tribal groups on the basis of 'Buggins' turn', was expecting a change of leadership at this level. Massimov was appointed to the highest political office below the President in 2007 at the age of 42. He is now Kazakhstan's longest serving Prime Minister. After four years and three months in office – a period which coincided with the worst effects of the world recession – it was widely anticipated that he would move on. Nazarbayev had a more meritocratic perspective. He saw Massimov not only as the pilot who weathered the storm but as a co-navigator for the future. Nazarbayev trusts Massimov because he is a modernizer with a forward looking agenda for the domestic side of the reformed government.

'We will be paying much more attention to education particularly to the teaching of English language', said Massimov when I asked him what his priorities would be. 'We have to shift upwards to the highest requirements of international competitiveness, using American and European standards. Of course we are a Central Asian country, but taking Singapore as our model we are aiming for best international practice in healthcare, ecology and criminal justice reform.'

When he makes such promises, Massimov is aware of his own accountability for he is no stranger to political criticism. Unlike the President, who is constitutionally protected as head of state from personalized attacks in the media, the Prime Minister has to engage in much more of the rough and tumble of arguments on the internet, even in response to negative comments on his own blog.

'I strongly believe in the freedoms that are created by the internet', says Massimov. 'I am giving priority to the development of high speed broadband internet connectivity. It will bring more freedom of expression and more competitiveness. The country with the highest broadband speed in the world today is South Korea with 16 megabytes. The USA comes second with 8 megabytes. Today in Kazakhstan our broadband speed is 2 megabytes but within three years we will be equal to South Korea at the top of the international league.'

Massimov's enthusiasm for internet-led modernisation is shared by many of the ministers and deputy ministers in his team. They tend to be technocrats rather than politicians and they are sensitive to the currents of public opinion that emerge from New Kazakhstan's internet generation. Political strategy is not their remit. 'Pass. You've come to the wrong address', said one senior minister when I started to ask him questions about democratic values and constitutional reforms.

Reform is nevertheless in the air as the twentieth anniversary milestone is passed. Now that the economy is growing again, the first priority is spreading the national wealth more evenly. That means attacking the bad habits of Old Kazakhstan corruption. It also involves opening up property rights, share ownership and incentives for starting new businesses to the young and ambitious. In his inauguration speech five days after the election, President Nazarbayev spoke of 'establishing the foundations of "people's capitalism"'. The first stage of the process will be "people's IPOs". They will initiate the process of high quality privatisation'.

As this new money trickles downwards, it should release political as well as economic energy. 'We must develop the political culture', declared Nazarbayev in the same inaugural address. He did not say how or when this development would take place. However there was a clear hint that its first phase would be consensual rather than adversarial. For the President was pleased that his re-election had taken place without what he called 'black PR'. By this he did not mean that the opposition had been silenced, for those with good hearing could tune in to the murmurings of criticism among the electorate even though they were not reflected at the ballot box. More likely, Nazarbayev was referring to the fact that the political debate had been conducted in an atmosphere of civility, or as he put it: 'without harsh confrontation'.

Perhaps those last three words point to the manner in which Old Kazakhstan and New Kazakhstan disagreed over the referendum. There was a confrontation but a calm one. The disagreement was handled with wisdom. Some might call the referendum that became an election an example of returning to the ancient Khanate tradition of listening to the tribes and then acting in the nation's best interests. Others could claim that it was a more futuristic approach of responding to the populist pressures of the day. But the end result set a precedent, enabling Nazarbayev to say in his inaugural address: 'This should be an example for all future election campaigns. Only in this case will we develop a real democracy, an effective multiparty system and a system of free and responsible media'.

These were not empty promises even though they had no timetable. For Nazarbayev knows that the demographic clock is ticking. A young increasingly well educated country with an average age of 31 is not going to stand still on political reform even though economic success and stability remains their highest priority. Perhaps the most emotional sentence in the inaugural speech came when the President said, 'The active participation of youngsters in the election and their support moved me to tears'. It was clear that these words came from his heart. For he is on the side of New Kazakhstan even though he has to balance its demands with the more traditional interests of Old Kazakhstan. Nazarbayev, who has watched developments in the Arab world with close attention knows he is leading his country from autocracy to democracy at a speed which no faction and no individual can control. The pace of progress will be decided by the unfolding events of twenty-first history.

So far, Kazakhstan is ahead of the curve of progress in its own region and in the wider Islamic world. This is a tolerant, secular and economically successful society. It cannot be compared to Egypt, Libya, Syria, Bahrain or any other repressed nation which had featured in the 'Arab spring' uprisings of 2011. Although Kazakhstan's political reforms need further development, the wider reforms of the country's institutions and social practices are gathering momentum. A surprising example of this reforming tendency is to be found in what used to be the worst arena of Kazakhstan's Soviet inheritance – the criminal justice system.

3

Reforming the Law

A Journey into Kazakhstan's Criminal Justice System

(I) JOURNEY INTO PRISONS

My journey into Kazakhstan's criminal justice system began at the bottom – in the prisons. They were quite a surprise because of changes now taking place both inside and outside their walls.

I would never have entered the world of incarceration in Kazakhstan had it not been for an unexpected conversation with President Nazarbayev in 2008. We were at the end of an interviewing session. Having answered all my questions at that stage of the biography he asked: 'What else are you doing in your life besides writing this book about me?'

'I am chairing a report on the reform of British prisons and the rehabilitation of offenders'. I replied.[1]

'That's just what we need here!' exclaimed the President. 'Would you go and look at our prisons and report on them for us? We have far too many people in jail. We need to find some alternative way of punishing them'.

The President then told a story, which I have since heard from others who were present, about his visit to a court in Balkhash a few weeks earlier. In the dock were two young men, both with previous convictions, accused of stealing a stereo player valued at $100, from a car. After they were found guilty, the judge asked the offenders if they could pay compensation to the owner of the stereo. They replied that they were unemployed and had no money. The prosecutor said in that case he demanded a prison sentence of not less than three years.

At this point the President of the Republic of Kazakhstan stood up in the public gallery.

'Why are you being so tough?' he asked the prosecutor, 'these are young guys, without a job and the value of the stolen property is low. Surely they could get a penalty that would be less than 3 years in prison – some training or something?'

In consternation, the prosecutor replied that under the penal code Kazakhstan had inherited from the Soviet Union the law required at least a 3 year prison sentence for previous offenders who were not offering compensation to the victim of their crime.

'Then I will pay the compensation', declared the President. After his aides had produced $100, the judge (who dryly observed that this was an unusual intervention in the procedures of his court) gave the young men a suspended sentence to do work in the community. Subsequently the Akim or mayor of Balkhash received a request from the Presidential office that these offenders should be assigned to work which involved technical training. They have not been in trouble again since.

This not quite everyday story of a Presidential day out in court made a considerable impact on Nazarbayev to judge by his lively description of the scene. 'It just shows that there is far too much of the old Soviet system in our law enforcement agencies', he said. 'We must decrease the number of people in prison. Rehabilitation is a good idea for us. Please will you report to me and our Minister of Justice on how to get this done'.

A couple of months later I set off on my first tour of Kazakhstan's jails accompanied by 37 year old Marat Beketayev, the Vice Minister of Justice responsible for the committee of prison administration. I could not have found a more interesting and sympathetic companion.

Beketayev is representative of the new breed of Kazakh officialdom, far removed in his thinking and his managerial abilities from the 'old guard' ways of those who were trained by Moscow. His father, originally an apple grower, fell on hard times and joined the prison service to earn a monthly salary in a job that offered official accommodation. As a result, the Beketayev family grew up in the village of Zarechny which was the centre of an agricultural penal colony.

Marat Beketayev won his way by scholarships from his village school to Almaty University. He learned to speak good English on a course offered by the British Council. After a spell in business he entered the civil service. As he rose through the ranks of the government, his father warned him never to mention that he had grown up in Zarechny because people might assume that he was the son of a convict.

Far from being a disadvantage, Beketayev's upbringing near a penal colony gave him an understanding of prison life which became useful when the new Ministry of Justice was formed as a separate government department. Unusually for a prison's minister he had a genuine interest in the rehabilitation of offenders. So that was how the connection was made between the Vice Minister and the British author with an interest in the same subject.

We arrived at the first port of call on our tour which was Granitny jail in Kokchetau province. My heart sank at its outward appearance. In Soviet times Kazakhstan was the heartland of the *gulag*, that sinister network of isolated penal camps immortalized in the books of Aleksandr Solzhenitsyn. He served his years of incarceration in a northern Kazakhstan prison almost identical to the one I was now entering.

Seen from the outside, Kazakhstan's jails look grim and antiquated. Most of them were built in the Soviet era. Their external architecture (if it can be called that) created such ugly monoliths that they resemble featureless corpses embalmed in a carapace of crumbling walls. Their general state of dilapidation and rusty iron bars created an air of pervasive sadness. Yet once you enter these former gulag fortresses there can be positive discoveries.

The first surprise is that Kazakhstan's prisons are noticeably tidier and cleaner than many of their British and American equivalents. This goes beyond the showpiece spotlessness which can be contrived for an inspection. Having been a former prisoner and jail cleaner myself I know where to look for nooks and crannies of uncleanliness. When my experienced eye focused on the lower rims of toilet bowls, the tiles behind the showers and waste pipes under kitchen sinks, Kazakh prisons could not be faulted for lack of spit, polish and disinfectant. A key factor here may be fear of infection, for TB is a problem in many of the country's jails. But whatever the cause, a clean prison is a sign of a well run prison.

A second surprise was the amount of space and the amount of staff effort allocated to conjugal visits. Every jail in Kazakhstan has a substantial accommodation block where wives and families can come to stay, sometimes for several days. Although petty corruption among prison officers is often an ingredient in the arrangements for such family sojourns, nevertheless the principle of prisoner entitlement to conjugal visits is firmly established in national law and practice. Since such rights do not exist in most Western countries, including Britain, I asked why they were given priority in Kazakhstan.

'Because without them many prisoners would be divorced and would never know their children', replied a Granitny officer, barely able to conceal his astonishment at such a silly question from a foreigner, 'we think it is an important part of our job to help families stay together'.

There are other dimensions of humanity in Kazakhstan's jails, for example, an emphasis on disease prevention and medical care. But the prevailing characteristics seem to be excessive bureaucracy and over-disciplined militarism. Endless rules and notices, time tables of dietary information designating how many grams of fish a prisoner will get for lunch the Friday after next; and a preponderance of uniforms and parades are integral parts of the system. There is an element of class distinction in that white collar criminals, particularly ex-civil servants who have committed offences such as fraud and corruption are sent to special jails, in Astana or Semipalatinsk where the regime is lighter. But particularly since the prisons were moved away from the Ministry of the Interior (a feared symbol of Soviet rule) to the jurisdiction of the new Ministry of Justice in 2005 there have been many quiet improvements in the country's 70 jails, which at the time of my first visit held 63,000 inmates.

I have visited eight prisons in Kazakhstan. As a result of recommendations made after my first tour of three jails in August 2009, Marat Beketayev and his team at the Prisons Committee launched rehabilitation programmes in five correctional institutions in the Akmolinsk region. I was invited back to see how these pilot schemes were working in February 2010. With Soren Johnson, the Russian-speaking executive vice president of Prison Fellowship International (PFI), who travelled from Washington DC, we toured prisons around Astana, Kokchetau and Stepnogorsk. Despite the arctic external conditions of our journey, inside the jails we were impressed by the dedication of the pilot scheme teachers who were giving the young offenders up to eight hours a day of instruction on courses such as motor vehicle repairing, welding, cooking and English language.

Although the workshop facilities for some of these courses were antique by modern standards, the prisoners on the programme were on target to achieve vocational certificates in areas where there are skill shortages in Kazakhstan, particularly in the energy sector. At one prison 80 inmates were going out each morning into day release employment in the private sector. At another there was a promising scheme for placing about-to-be released prisoners in jobs with local companies. Such green shoots of rehabilitation are an encouraging development.

I have not looked at Kazakhstan's prisons through rose coloured spectacles. Thanks to the transparency and candour of the briefings I have been given I know that many unacceptable features remain. There is still too much minor corruption among and some occasional brutality by, a minority of prison officers.

There is also an unspoken division of the system into red and black jails. The former are institutions controlled by the prison staff. The latter are controlled by the inmates, specifically gang leaders. The red and black categories are old Soviet designations. They are steadily being eliminated by a new generation of pro-active prison governors such as the energetic Kasym Umirov who I first met in Kokchetau. He has since been promoted to run the country's number one jail in Astana.

Throughout Kazakhstan, attitudes to prison and prisoners are changing. Thanks to the internet, abuses are flushed out into the open with greater transparency. Systemic torture within prisons has been eradicated, as the next section of this chapter indicates. Rehabilitation is moving up on the agenda and the number of inmates is coming down.

Kazakhstan began life as an independent nation with one of the highest prison counts in the world (over 100,000) in relation to its population of 16 million. When I made my first visit to a Kazakh jail in 2009 the inmate total was over 63,000. Today it is 49,000 and Today it is 49,000 and falling thanks to policy changes and new legislation decriminalising many offences.

However President Nazarbayev remains a critic of his own

government's administration of the prison system. In many of the red jails described in an earlier paragraph the power of the gangs was becoming greater than the authority of the prison officers. As a result there was much smuggling of drugs, weapons, cell phones and other forbidden items. More disturbingly there were many escapes of armed prisoners in 2010–11 causing a loss of confidence in the penitentiary management committee of the Ministry of Justice.

In July 2011 Nazarbayev responded to the public disquiet about prisons by issuing a Presidential Decree which announced a crackdown on the country's worst jails. The administration of the penitentiary system was transferred away from the Ministry of Justice back to the Ministry of Internal Affairs. This move was accompanied by public assurances that Kazakhstan would continue to uphold a number of UN, EU and OSCE recommendations which guaranteed minimum standards for the humane treatment of prisoners and outlawed torture or degrading punishments.

Looked at in the round there are clearly tensions in the prisons between the reform agenda and the 'get tough' agenda. But the arguments involved are not a one way street. From the point of view of reducing prison numbers and improving human rights there has been genuine progress. One interesting area in which the old stereotypes of Soviet style criminal justice have been replaced by new humanitarian improvements concerns the issue of torture.

*   *   *

(II) QUESTIONS OF TORTURE

In 2009, a draft UN report alleged that torture was 'systemic' in Kazakhstan prisons and that one particular jail, Zhetygara was notorious for being 'the Guantanamo of Kazakhstan'. In fact, the report was wrong on both counts and contained a substantial number of other errors. In the face of vigorous representatives from the Ministry of Justice in Astana, the draft had to be amended, not least by making the important

correction that torture was *'not systemic'* in the country's penal establishments. The Guantanamo comparison was also withdrawn.

Although these changes amounted to a significant climb down by
the UN Rapporteur, Dr Manfred Nowak, who wrote the initial report,
the Kazakh officials most concerned with these issues were careful not
to claim a major victory. For the fact of the matter was that regrettable
episodes of torture had occasionally occurred within certain prisons. So
the Ministry of Justice launched a drive to eliminate these bad practices
and invited Dr Nowak to come and see for himself what had been
achieved. The consequence was a remarkably open public debate with
an end result that showed both the UN and the Ministry of Justice in
a good light. The story is an illuminating example of how twenty-first
century Kazakhstan can change for the better.

The seventy-three page Nowak report, issued in draft form in
September 2009, detailed several specific allegations of torture in
Kazakhstan jails particularly in Stepnogorsk prison hospital in
Zhetygara penitentiary. The Kazakh authorities were shocked by the
UN Rapporteurs' findings and produced a detailed analysis of them
under the supervision of Vice Minister Marat Beketayev and Deputy
Prosecutor General Askhat Daulbayev.

This analysis showed that while some of the Rapporteurs' criticisms
were valid, others were invalid. A weakness of the UN findings was
that they relied heavily on hearsay evidence which came from third
parties who had never visited the prisons criticized in the report. The
Kazakhs took particular exception to the implication that Stepnogorsk
was a torture facility rather than a genuine hospital and that Zhetygara
deserved to be called the 'Guantanamo of Kazakhstan'.

In the formal rebuttal he prepared to deliver to the UN General
Assembly, Marat Beketayev attacked the emotive Guantanamo
comparison as manifestly unfair because the US prison of that name
was holding terrorist suspects who had never been put on trial whereas
Zhetygara was a jail for inmates who had been tried and convicted by
the courts of wide ranging criminal offences. The Vice Minister also
exposed a more fundamental flaw in the Guantanamo label.

'It is absolutely wrong to use such a metaphor in an important report', said Beketayev, 'all the more so considering that the Special Rapporteur himself did not visit that facility and used the comparison made to him by persons who had been held in other institutions and who had never been to that facility'.

Faced with the evidence of these and other flaws in his report the UN Rapporteur discussed them at meetings in Vienna and Geneva in early 2010 with Beketayev and Daulbayev.

'Basically we were telling him in a polite way that he had made some bad mistakes', recalled Beketayev, 'so we said to him in effect we will not dwell on them in our reply. We do not want an escalation and we hope you will accept our invitation to come back to Kazakhstan to see how we are improving the situation'.

As a result of these discussions Dr Nowak made an emollient speech to the UN General Assembly's Human Rights Council on 8 March 2010 in Geneva, praising the Kazakhstan government for its co-operation and declaring that torture was 'not systemic' in the country's prisons. This was true by early 2010 for the Ministry of Justice had by then issued a series of directions to police and prison officers prohibiting them from using any form of torture; produced a detailed action plan with nineteen instructions setting up preventative mechanisms against torture; and establishing a series of anti-torture guidelines for prosecutors and judges. The purpose of this exercise was to ensure that Kazakhstan was fully compliant with the recommendations of the UN's 2008 Convention on Torture.

In the autumn of 2010, Dr Manfred Nowak returned to Kazakhstan and visited several prisons of his choice. A public conference on torture and cruel and unusual punishment was held in Astana attended by over 40 specialist observers from local and international NGO's including Freedom House, the Helsinki Committee and Human Rights Watch. There was an open debate with speeches from the Vice Minister of Justice, the Deputy Prosecutor General and the UN Special Rapporteur. Some of the abuse cases were acknowledged as serious past mistakes by individual officers within the system. It was generally agreed that real progress had been made by the country in making torture illegal and unacceptable.

One Western Ambassador who attended the forum said afterwards: 'There was a true sense of engagement and it was something of a role model event showing the way forward on how human rights issues can be well handled both by the Kazakhstan authorities and their human rights critics. The end result of all these exchanges is that torture is clearly now illegal within the criminal justice system of this country.'

* * *

(III) THE PROBLEM OF CORRUPTION

The Prosecutor General and the Minister of the Interior are the two most important law enforcement officers in Kazakhstan. I interviewed both of them for this book to understand their respective roles in government and to assess how they are tackling one of the most troublesome problems of Kazakhstan's society – corruption.

Kairat Mami, who until 2009 was Chief Justice of the Supreme Court, is Prosecutor General of Kazakhstan. The fact that he was promoted from the former post to his present office is an illustration of the primacy of his importance in his country's criminal justice system. By international comparison his role approximates to that of the US Attorney-General or to the UK's Director of the Crown Prosecution Service.

Kairat Mami's department has a staff of 4,900 and is responsible for all prosecutions across the country – an annual total of 47,000 cases. Of these only 3 per cent result in acquittals. When asked if this figure was unfairly low, Mami explained that a further 15 per cent of cases are dropped before coming to court because Kazakhstan's legal process tests the strength of the prosecution and defence evidence in pre-trial procedures that bear some resemblance to the French *juge d'instruction* preliminary hearings.

In his presentation of a prosecution system in transition, Kairat Mami explained that the decriminalization of many offences by the President and Parliament in 2010–11 was reducing the workload of his department. 'We inherited our penal code from the era of the Soviets and a lot of their laws and punishments have been hibernating in our statutes ever since', he explained. 'Some of the penalties were far too tough. For example, if a market trader was caught cheating a customer with false weights he was sent to jail. Now we have changed this and about fifty other laws so that these offences can be settled by civil procedures such as a compensation agreement between buyer and seller. Also we have softened many other penalties for minor offenders. Instead of custodial sentences they now are fined or made to do work in the community'.

When asked about drug offences, Kairat Mami asked an aide to bring in a chart setting out the new tariffs for sentences. It showed that there had been no change in the long jail terms for sellers of drugs. But those in possession of small quantities of marijuana were now treated leniently with warnings or fines. In the case of those addicted to hard drugs they were now sent for forty days or so to a treatment facility and not to prison. 'We no longer allow the police to score a statistic for a crime solved if they bust a small time addict', said the Prosecutor General.

I asked Kairat Mami about the prosecution and sentence of Yevgeny Zhovtis. This case has in recent months been top of the list of the concerns of human rights organizations such as Freedom House who scrutinize Kazakhstan. At the prompting of those organizations and the State Department, President Obama, in a Blair House meeting on 11 April 2010 asked President Nazarbayev if he would review the Zhovtis sentence? Nazarbayev refused, saying it had been correctly dealt with by the courts.

The basic facts of this case are not in dispute. Zhovtis, a well known Almaty lawyer, was driving a car late at night when he hit and killed a pedestrian. Alcohol was not involved. There were said to be other mitigating circumstances, particularly an offer by Zhovtis to pay compensation, colloquially known as 'blood money', to the dead man's family. In such cases the courts often accept the compensation arrangement and do not demand a custodial penalty. In the Zhovtis case however a four year prison sentence was imposed. Washington human rights campaigner, notably Sam Patten of Freedom House, alleged that Yevgeny Zhovtis was jailed only because he himself was a well known human rights lawyer and activist.

This argument was answered in detail when I put it to Prosecutor General Kairat Mami.

'I looked carefully into this case myself because of the attention it received in the West and I am 100 per cent certain that the investigating team and the court acted correctly,' he said. 'First of all there is no doubt that Zhovtis was at fault. He was driving too fast on a dark and dangerous stretch of road which animals and people were known to cross. He should have been driving slower. He killed a local man walking near his home who was not in the least to blame for the accident. Even Zhovtis and his lawyers accepted this.'

'Secondly, although the dead man's sister accepted the compensation offer, the dead man's mother did not accept it. When she refused it and walked out of the court, Zhovtis was asked by the judge what he wanted to say and he started to argue very stubbornly. He actually said, "Although I regret this accident I do not feel guilty about it". Our courts expect a defendant in such cases to accept their responsibility and to express a contrite apology. So it was not a surprise that a prison sentence was passed'.

Asked if a four year jail term had been passed to keep Zhovtis from his human rights activities, as Freedom Housed claimed, during the year of Kazakhstan's OSCE Presidency, Kairat Mami replied:

'I like and respect Zhovtis. We often appeared as professional lawyers in the same court together and we sometimes spoke at the same international conferences. He expressed a point of view about certain changes needed in our system but he was never hostile towards Kazakhstan, in fact I think he was good for Kazakhstan. So his views were nothing to do with his sentence which was the same as most others. He is now in a detention colony – not a strict prison – with other drivers who have caused deaths. They are serving three, four or five year sentences. Zhovtis was not treated any differently because of his opinions as a human rights lawyer. I am sorry he is in detention but that is our law'.

My last question to the Prosecutor General, a former Chief Justice of the Supreme Court, was about the independence of Kazakhstan's judiciary.

'In constitutional terms our judiciary can never be 100 per cent independent of the state, for it is there to support and serve the interests of the state which created it', said Kairat Mami, 'but what I can say is that our judges do not take orders from anyone above them. They are the most highly paid of all officials, receiving salaries of approximately $4,000 to $5,000 a month, and they cannot be removed from their positions. I can confidently claim that our judiciary is no longer influenced by phone calls from Akims (mayors) or Ministers. Judges give their own opinions and judgements on cases before them and they are not changed by outside pressures or corruptions'.

Fighting corruption has moved high up on the agenda of both the Prosecutor General and the Minister of Interior, Serik Baimaganbetov, whom I also interviewed later on the same day. This is a battle which needs to be fought vigorously. Most independent observers of Kazakhstan agree that corruption is a rampant problem in the country from the highest official levels, through middle class professionals such as teachers awarding exam grades down to lowly traffic cops handing out speeding tickets.

Asked about corruption among the 77,000 police officers under his control (24,000 of whom are armed) Interior Minister Serik Baimaganbetov spoke frankly.

'Yes, there is a corruption problem in my department but it is not endemic and we are having a lot of success in reducing it. New technology is playing an important part in minimizing corruption among Highway Patrol officers these days', he said, running through a list of gadgetry that ranged from radar speed guns, to video cameras on traffic cars, to police voice recorders and a centralized CCTV control room in big cities which recorded the movements and dialogue with suspects of patrol officers. Also IT systems were now in place which would eliminate much of the petty corruption in the Ministry of the Interior over the issuing of many forms of licenses and permits.

I asked why the anti-corruption drive was only hitting the little guys and failing to catch the big fish. Both senior officials denied the suggestion. Prosecutor General Mami ran though a list of corrupt VIPs his department had brought to justice in the last two years. They included two senior ministers, two heads of important government agencies, three Akims and some bankers.

The picture I was given by both the Minister of the Interior and the Prosecutor General is of a criminal justice system in which sweeping reforms are under way, accountability is strengthening and crime is being held in check with serious crimes of violence down by 12 per cent in 2008–10. The most obvious manifestations of these changes are the reduction in the number of jail places and the cutting back in the criminal powers of law enforcement agencies whose functions often overlapped and went too far.

On the first of these two areas, an earlier section of this chapter reported from inside the prisons on the improvements and the fall in inmate totals. Even so it was remarkable to hear the leadership of the criminal justice system talking with such enthusiasm about setting prisoners free and improving Kazakhstan's ratings in the international league tables of jail populations.

'In our jails this morning we had 49,299 inmates', said Prosecutor General Kairat Mami flourishing an overnight report from the Ministry of Justice. 'This is itself already a big reduction from twelve months ago. Thanks to our decriminalization of offences legislation we expect to see a further 3,000 prisoners released almost immediately and thanks to our softer sentences I predict that we will soon be seeing another twelve to fifteen per cent cut in the number of inmates.'

'When I look at the international comparisons of prison populations per thousand of each country's overall national populations I see that Kazakhstan is rated as having the twenty-third highest number of prisoners in the world. I now expect us to improve that rating by falling by ten or more places in those league tables.'

It is certainly a surprise to hear of such results from the current criminal justice reforms in a country that was once a police state and whose detractors still accuse it of being one. But to paraphrase a combination of Bob Dylan, Elvis Presley and Chuck Berry 'the-times-they-are-a-changin' in twenty-first century Kazakhstan. The leading criminal justice agencies are getting all shook up. And the most symbolic establishment where there's a whole lotta shakin' goin' on, would you believe it, is the KGB.

*   *   *

(IV) INSIDE THE KGB

The KGB casts a long shadow of fear in any country that was once part of the Soviet Union. Kazakhstan is no exception to this history of bad memories. For most of the last twenty years it has maintained a powerful security apparatus, many of whose 12,000 secret police operatives were trained in the methods and mindset of KGB from its notorious headquarters in Dzerzhinsky Square, Moscow. Even though the organization has now changed its name from KGB to KNB (Kazakhstan National Security Bureau) most Kazakhstanis do not look on it in a user friendly light. Some of them dislike it even more intensely because in recent years the KNB (still widely called the KGB) has extended its reach to mundane areas of wrongdoing such as tax evasion, customs violations and ordinary crimes. So many additional citizens in Kazakhstan have been getting the dreaded knock on the door from the KNB and experiencing its interrogations.

Yet like every other law enforcement agency in the country the KGB or KNB is undergoing scrutiny, reform and change as never before. It says something for the organizations new transparency that as a foreign author I found it comparatively easy to arrange a visit to the KNB's headquarters in Astana and to conduct an on the record interview with its recently appointed Chairman. It is hard to imagine such easy access being granted to a writer, complete with tape recorder by the current heads of MI5, MI6 or the CIA. When I remarked on this accessibility when walking across the courtyard of the KNB's main building my escort replied, 'Yes, you are right. These days our Chairman gets quite a lot of foreign visitors. We are more open now'.

Considering it is the nerve centre of the country's internal and external security the KNB does not have the atmosphere of a closed or oppressive fortress. Its headquarters are a modern rectangular office block built in highly polished grey granite. Protected only by a single perimeter iron fence, the KNB is located in a fashionable district of downtown Astana, adjacent to a prestigious local school and overlooked by an ornately designed Chinese hotel. It is easy to find because of the large KNB signs on the front wall of the building. The security checks at the entrance are thorough but not nearly as intrusive as the procedures for a visitor going into the CIA at Langley or the SIS at Vauxhall Cross. No body searches, fingerprinting, digital photography or X-rays are deemed necessary in Astana.

Walking through the entrance hall, a rare photograph of President Nazarbayev in full military uniform is on display. It is a reminder that the KNB is constitutionally part of the armed forces of which the President is Commander-in-Chief.

Along the walls of the airy first floor corridor hang formal photographs of previous KNB committee chairmen, mostly in uniform. After a brief wait in a comfortably furnished outer office, I am ushered into the inner sanctum of the present Chairman. After handshakes and preliminary greetings I ask if I can tape record my interview with him. 'Certainly you can, you are most welcome to do so', he replied.

The Chairman of the KNB is Nurtai Abikayev, the President's most trusted and long serving counsellors. For many years he was Nazarbayev's chief of staff, a post he first held as early as the mid 1980's when his boss was a somewhat isolated political figure as a puppet Prime Minister of the Soviet Republic of Kazakhstan with only limited powers devolved from Moscow.

In more recent years Abikayev has been Kazakhstan's Ambassador to Russia (the country's top diplomatic appointment) and First Deputy Foreign Minister. His appointment to the key role of Chairman of the KNB in 2010 came as a surprise to Astana watchers. Some of them regarded it as a retrograde step by Nazarbayev. They predicted that this promotion of an 'old guard' crony from the President's inner circle would usher in a new era of tighter security clampdowns. These forecasts were wrong.

Nurtai Abikayev was appointed by the President to be the new broom who would carry out a programme of sweeping reforms. He has been tasked with selling these reforms to the security establishment. He also chairs a key committee of heads of law enforcement agencies with a mandate to ensure that the changes the President wants are implemented swiftly and without overlapping rivalries between competing bureaucracies.

Nurtai Abikayev is an urbane and attractive figure with matinee idol good looks (think of Rex Harrison or Cary Grant in mid-career). He is charming, outgoing and informative, light years removed from the fictional Soviet-era spymasters like Karla of the John le Carre novels or Blofeld of Ian Fleming's *Smersh*. Although Abikayev speaks only Russian, he is westernized in outlook. One of his sons is an international rally driver, his grandson goes to Harrow, his daughter lives in London and is married to a director of Christies. He appears to enjoy answering questions about his job and the new priorities he is giving to it.

'Our committee is returning to the original mission of our secret service which is safeguarding the national security of Kazakhstan', says Abikayev. 'Unfortunately major mistakes were made by my predecessors. Last year ninety per cent of the KNB's investigations were into matters which had nothing to do with national security. They should have been dealt with by the police, the customs or the tax authorities. So I have redefined our priorities and tightened up our internal discipline to stop these mistakes. From now on the KNB concentrates only on the areas that affect our security such as fighting international terrorism, preventing major drug trafficking, stopping illegal migration and defecting plots by religious extremists'. Asked how the KNB drew the line between religious freedom and religious extremism, Chairman Abikayev answered:

'Under our constitution any citizen can pray to any God he or she wants. We encourage this freedom, and after the collapse of the Soviet

Union we welcome spiritual values coming back into our society. From Islam we were happy that people have set up the Spiritual Council of Muslims of Kazakhstan. But we never thought that religious extremism would be brought in to this country from outside organizations who have brainwashed some of our young people and turned them into fanatics who follow extreme forms of Wahhabism and Sufism or join Hizb-ut-Tahrir. Of course it is a big challenge for us to distinguish between the peaceful and the extreme followers of religion. This is delicate work, but we have had some success at it'.

The success to which Chairman Abikayev was referring was the foiling of a terrorist bomb plot in November 2010 by an organization called Kazakh Jamaat. As he described it:

'On the eve of the OSCE summit we arrested a group of people thanks to information received from our American colleagues in the CIA. The leader of this group was a disaffected former law enforcement officer who wanted to undermine our government. This man accepted his guilt and co-operated fully with us. With his help we found a store of ammunition and explosives in Almaty which was about to be used to blow up government buildings in that city, in Astana and for some reason in Temirtau. So we prevented their bombings just in time. Normally we keep quiet about our successes as a security organization but some of this story leaked into the press so I can speak about it'.

The story of the OSCE bombings that were foiled by the KNB is a reminder that Central Asia can be a dangerous place. Abikayev believes that the major threats to Kazakhstan's national security came from external sources. There is huge volatility in the region coming from trouble making organizations which include the Taliban, the Chechnya Liberation Front, the Uighur secessionist movement and various armed splinter groups in unstable neighbouring countries such as Kyrgyzstan, Uzbekistan and Iran. To this noxious mixture should be added the drug smugglers operating in and out of Turkey, Russia or Afghanistan and the religious fanatics from the wilder realms of Islamist extremism. Under Nurtai Abikayev's leadership, today's KNB has become leaner in size, reducing its central staff by fifteen per cent although its border guards have increased in certain places to deal with increased pressures. The most fundamental change is that the organization no longer concerns itself with domestic crimes that are unrelated to national security. So even if the bad memories and mistakes of predecessor Chairmen take a long time to fade, a new and better course has been set for the KNB in twenty-first century Kazakhstan.

*   *   *

(V) LAW REFORMER-IN-CHIEF

No new course is set in Kazakhstan without the approval of President Nazarbayev. This is doubly true in the case of strategic and sensitive state organizations like the KNB, the Ministry of the Interior, the Ministry of Justice, the Prisons Committee, the Customs, the Financial Police and the Prosecutor General's Office. As the earlier sections of this chapter make clear all these law enforcement agencies are being reformed at a speed and scale that has surprised most Kazakhstanis. What is happening and why?

Some months before these reforms were fully unveiled Nazarbayev spoke frankly in an interview for this book about his frustrations over the law and order practices of his government:

'There's still too much of the old Soviet system in our law enforcement agencies. The delays between the various authorities on, say, drug testing cases are intolerable. The KNB are involved, the Customs are involved, the Police are involved but none of them want to take the final responsibility. We have too many officials who just play on the nerves of the ordinary citizens with their long investigations. So we will simplify the system and decriminalize many offences. We will use administrative sanctions and financial penalties rather than custodial sentences. My objective is to bring about a significant decrease in the number of people in prison'.

At the time of this interview I was privately sceptical as to whether these Presidential objectives would be achieved. Now I know better. From the top of the KGB to the bottom of the prison system, Nazarbayev's new brooms are sweeping out old malpractices and bringing in new changes. Inevitably there is resistance within the bureaucracies. On 17 January 2011, the President called a meeting in the Ministry of the Interior at which he gave his law enforcement chiefs a sharp dressing down about the lack of progress in their implementation of his reform agenda. If his privately expressed impatience was not enough, Nazarbayev reinforced his views publicly with this remarkable passage in the State of the Nation speech he delivered to Parliament on January 28 2011:

'Let there be no doubt about the importance of this programme which will result in over 2,000 prisoners being released from jail in the next few months ...

And let there be no doubt about our determination to fight against corruption. No one is above the law. As part of our anti-corruption drive the Minister of Health is now in jail! The Minister for the Environment in jail! The head of the Atomic Energy Company (Kazatomprom) is in jail! The Chairman of the Land Property Department in the Ministry of Agriculture is in jail! Some county Akims are in jail! There will be no compromises in our fight against corruption.'

As I watched the President deliver this strong message in his State of the Nation address, my view from the gallery encompassed a range of emotions among the assembled audience of Senators, MPs, and Ministers. They were thrown by the unexpected vigour of Nazarbayev's words. Some of them seemed to be wondering whether or not they should applaud this exclamatory roll call of Ministers behind bars. Others shifted uneasily in their seats at this reminder of the fate of former colleagues. One or two looked alarmed, perhaps with worry that their names might be next on the list. All appeared to be waking up to an understanding that the era of greased palms, high level favours, pork barrel politics and even outright corruption might be coming towards its end.

Eliminating the widespread levels of corrupt practices in Kazakhstani society will not be achieved by one Presidential speech or even perhaps by one President. But real change in this unattractive area of the nation's life is beginning to happen and the President is driving it hard. What are the influences propelling him into this new role of Kazakhstan's Law Reformer in Chief?

The first influence is that Nazarbayev is a good listener. He knows that there is unease at all levels of society about the extent of bribe taking and bribe making, even within the law enforcement agencies themselves as well as within ministries and state owned corporations. Sometimes this phenomenon of daily life is greeted with resigned shrugs, sometimes with barbed humour and occasionally with outrage. For example, at the start of the Asian Winter Games which Kazakhstan hosted in February 2011 it was announced that the cost of the project – from Olympic ice-rinks in Almaty, to a 15,000 seat stadium in Astana, to firework displays of spectacular extravagance – would cost $1.5 billion. It may have been well spent, but that's not what was being said by the spectators at the bars during the events. The sceptical opinion was that a good proportion of the Winter Games budget was ending up in corrupt pockets.

The President hears this scepticism. He does not want Kazakhstan to emulate modern Russia in being derided as one of the most notoriously corrupt countries of the world. So he is cleaning out the stables, making examples high and low and encouraging the powerful State Prosecutors department to pursue a zero-tolerance policy. It seems to be working, at least in changing the climate of public opinion towards corruption from tolerance to intolerance.

A second influence is that Nazarbayev knows that he has to move his country forward from the era of Soviet-style law enforcement. Perhaps it is not surprising that reforming prisons and police forces should not have been high on the agenda of a country that has been fighting for economic survival in many of its first 20 years of independence. But now that the lower regions of law and order have got the President's attention he is pleased to be cutting costs, abolishing unnecessary criminal statutes and even getting credit among his customary critics in the human rights NGOs for reducing jail population.

As for the changes in the KNB, Nazarbayev knows that this arm of the state security system exceeded its mandate with heavy handed expansionism in the last ten years. He has halted this and reversed the trend with the appointment of Nurtai Abikayev as Chairman. What is not widely known is that the President has his own personal and historical reasons for doing this.

During the 1980's, as Prime Minister of the Soviet Republic of Kazakhstan, Nazarbayev was twice put under surveillance and investigation by the KGB. The operations against him were political. He was becoming a thorn in the flesh of two successive First Secretaries, Dinmukhamed Kunayev and Gennady Kolbin who used the KGB as a means of clipping the wings of their ambitious potential successor.

Although the investigations came to nothing they were de-stabilizing and personally distressing to the rising star of Kazakh politics. Nazarbayev's closest aide at that time, the late Vladimir Ni, said of this period in a 2008 interview:

'This was one of the darkest hours of Nazarbayev's life. In the end he was completely vindicated. Even on some of the KGB's most petty allegations about expenses for groceries he was able to produce receipts (because I had kept them!)But there was no doubt that he was badly unsettled and then when the KGB investigated him again later he became ill. Deep down Nazarbayev does not like the methods of the KGB'.

These recollections may give an interesting insight into the President's current role as the reformer of the criminal justice system. When he says 'We have too many officials who just play on the nerves of ordinary citizens with their long investigations', this is a personal, as well as a political, observation.

What is also both personal and historical is Nazarbayev's desire to bequeath to his country and his own reputation the right legacy. He is not pleased with some of the western stereotypes which portray him as 'a dictator' who runs a 'police state'. But he may at least understand why such labels can be made to stick as long as the Soviet era inheritance of laws and law enforcement infrastructure remains in place. So there are legacy reasons why Nazarbayev has donned the mantle of Law Reformer-in-Chief with such surprising zeal and energy.

The changes that are now sweeping through the criminal justice system illustrate the truth of a widespread saying among Kazakhstanis: 'Nothing ever happens here unless *Papa* (The President) is making it happen'.

With this is mind, perhaps it is a good moment for a chapter in this book to attempt an answer to questions such as: Who is the President? Where did he come from? What has he achieved so far? And where is he going?

4

Understanding the President of Surprises

(I) CHARISMA AND COMPLEXITY

Nursultan Nazarbayev is full of surprises. They start with his physical presence. Anyone meeting him for the first time will soon have a powerful sense of the energy he radiates. If they have a conversation with him they will enjoy his charm. A good sense of humour, a physically fit appearance, an attractive personality, a gift for public speaking and a rapport with crowds are among his abilities. These would probably have enabled him to climb to the top or near to the top of the greasy pole of politics in many international societies, Western or Asian.

At a deeper level, Nazarbayev is hungry with intellectual curiosity. He absorbs facts and fresh ideas with the enthusiasm of a much younger politician. He likes to question his visitors so intensely that there are times when he seems to be a learner as much as a leader. These questions are often about matters far into the future, perhaps revealing glimpses of his sense of destiny. Yet his seriousness is balanced by a lightness of thought and touch, so a meeting with him often blends *gravitas* with *levitas*. These qualities combine to make him a charismatic but also a complex President. He is far removed from Western caricatures that portray him as the stern, unbending stereotype of a long serving Soviet era politician.

In terms of political longevity Nazarbayev does indeed go back a long time. He became a Komsomol or communist party youth leader in the early 1960s when John F Kennedy was in the White House and Nikita Khrushchev presided over the Kremlin. At the age of 44 he became the youngest Prime Minister of any republic in the Soviet Union and by 51 he was the First President of independent Kazakhstan. Throughout a career that has lasted for more than fifty years he has stayed consistently ahead of the curve. The break up of the Soviet Union, the rise of China, the emergence of Central Asian nationalism, the importance of whole hearted co-operation with the United States over nuclear weapons and the economic imperatives of oil and nuclear power to an energy hungry world were movements which Nazarbayev anticipated. He has steered his country through them with the skills of both a survivor and a strategist. He is nobody's political pawn. 'Never forget that Nazarbayev is a man of two cultures' said Mikhail Gorbachev in an interview with this author. 'He is both Russian and Asian in his roots and outlook.'

The personal complexity that has come from living in such close geographical proximity to China and Russia has served Nazarbayev well. He is a good neighbour but a determinedly independent one, subtle, rather than strident, when defending his country's interests.

His balancing act on the international scene has been complemented by similar dexterity when handling the competing interest groups at home. Kazakhstan is an ethnic melting pot with 138 nationalities, over 40 religions and over 30 languages[2]. Even its Kazakh majority contains many rivalries between tribes and regional groupings known as the Great, Middle and Small *zhuzs*. There are also tensions between old guard *apparatchiks* who were grounded in Soviet Culture and *avant-garde* young Kazakhstanis educated in the West. Among other factions are the rising middle classes, the long established family dynasties and assertive new oligarchs. Nazarbayev has mastered them all not so much by domination as by encouraging participation in the wealth of a growing economy. His Kazakhstan is an inclusive nation – provided you do not cross *Papa,* the nickname that is widely applied to him.

As President, Nazarbayev looks likely to remain in office long enough into the twenty-first century to see his country enjoying yet more growth in both geopolitical influence and economic riches. It is already the most important power in the volatile region of Central Asia. It is growing in international recognition, largely because it is on track to become one of the world's top ten oil producing nations. These achievements did not happen by accident. They might never have happened at all without Nazarbayev.

Political and economic leadership at this level requires many qualities, among them health, judgement, authority, industry, flexibility and vision. As a biographer and historian I have come to believe that Nazarbayev has the qualities to go on surprising his country and the world. To explain the reasons for this conclusion it is necessary to look both retrospectively and futuristically at the life, the record and the plans of the President of Kazakhstan.

* * *

(II) CHILDHOOD OF A TRUE KAZAKH

Nursultan Nazarbayev is first and last a true Kazakh. This two word label has deep meaning to the people he leads because their hearts and minds are rooted in the traditional culture of a nomadic inheritance.

For most of the eighteenth, nineteenth and twentieth centuries the Nazarbai family were nomads, roaming the steppes with their cattle until Stalinist decrees from Moscow forced Abish and Aljan Nazarbayev (Nursultan's parents) to become agricultural workers in a Soviet collective farm. The collective controlled vast grazing pastures around Ushkonyr (literally 'three brown hills'), a wild and beautiful expanse of *jailau* or upland meadows. In the first week of July 1940, somewhere on these *jailau*, Aljan Nazarbayeva began her labour pains. Because she and her husband had no home of their own at that time, there is considerable uncertainty as to the location and circumstances of their baby's arrival. Americans who like to romanticize about the humble birthplaces of their early Presidents as they travelled from 'log cabin to White House' would have difficulty in relating to the Kazakh version of this journey. For depending on which midwife's tale is accurate, the probability is that the future President of Kazakhstan was born on 6 July 1940 in the open air and open spaces of Ushkonyr. His neighbours in that wilderness were half a million sheep, cattle, wild horses and their herdsmen.

Although it would be impossible to imagine a more nomadic beginning to his life, the childhood of Nursultan Nazarbayev was moulded by a mixture of influences, both ancient and modern. On the ancient side he was brought up in the traditional Kazakh culture of reverence for ancestors, closeness to nature and bonding with the extended family of relatives who were his tribal kinsmen. On the modern side he was exposed to the new multi-ethnicity of races and religions that had been deported into twentieth century Kazakhstan from all over the Soviet Union. He was also a beneficiary of a new emphasis on education which had never before been part of his family's lifestyle.

Under the rules of the collective farm, Abish and Aljan Nazarbayev were allocated a half acre plot of land in the village of Chemolgan. On this plot they kept five sheep, twenty chickens, a horse and a cow. Abish was a hardworking smallholder with considerable skills at growing vegetables and grafting fruit trees. He managed to raise his family of four children on his plot, increasing his income by becoming a multi-lingual trader with the many ethnic groups displaced into this part of Kazakhstan by Stalin's purges.

Although the Soviet Union of Josef Stalin had many horrors, particularly for the oppressed Kazakhs, it established a better education system than most Westerners have acknowledged. So the young Nursultan Nazarbayev went to a good school in his home village Chemolgan. At the age of twelve he moved to a better one in the nearby town of Kaskelen. At both, he came top of his class getting A grades in all subjects with a particular aptitude for maths and physics. The deputy headmaster of Kaskelen School, Seitkhan Issayev, made an early assessment of him:

'I could see at once that Nazarbayev was the smartest boy in the tenth grade. He had an unusual thirst for knowledge asking me clever questions and often taking books away after class to read in the evenings. As often as not these books went wider than the curriculum. He wanted to learn more than the syllabus offered'.

The teenage Nazarbayev's enthusiasm for reading owed much to the encouragement he received at home. Although his parents were illiterate they believed passionately in education. They and other relatives in their extended family regularly bought books for the studious Nursultan when they made visits to the nearest city of Almaty. Usually these were Kazakh classics by authors such as Abay but as Nursultan's Russian improved he began reading authors such as Tolstoy, Chekhov and Pushkin. Later in his schooldays he devoured Russian translations of European authors, particularly enjoying the novels of Honoré de Balzac, Victor Hugo and Jules Verne.

Sometimes these literary interests seemed obsessive to other members of the Nazarbayev family. His younger brother Bolat remembers a scene in which their mother began shouting at the teenage Nursultan: 'You are reading too much. Your brain will boil. Get out into the fresh air!' The maternal order was obeyed – but only briefly. A few minutes later Nursultan stealthily climbed back into the house through a window and returned to his books.

As this anecdote suggests there were occasional tensions in the young Nazarbayev's life between homework and schoolwork. He escaped from them by reverting to his nomadic roots, particularly in the summer months. He developed a passion for climbing mountains, walking across the steppes and enjoying the wealth of nature to be found there. To this day the Alatau range around Ushkonyr is populated by many more wolves, mountain goats, deer, bears and snow leopards than human beings. Keeping such predators away from the collective farm's sheep and cattle was an important part of Abish's job as a herdsman. Nursultan remembers many idyllic moments of their father-son relationship when they were out in the wilds together, watching over the flocks at night, sitting round a camp fire singing folk songs to the music of a dombra – a traditional Kazakh lyre which the young boy learned to play well.

Kazakh traditions loomed large in the childhood of Nursultan Nazarbayev, among them the telling and re-telling of historic legends, the acceptance of tribal superstitions and the veneration of ancestors. Three non-traditional events also made an impact on his life. One was the death of Stalin, announced over loudspeakers to rural populations by communist party officials in 1953. Another was the installation of electricity in Chemolgan village in 1954. The third was a surprising letter arriving at Kaskelen school in 1957 from a Chinese student in Beijing, asking if anyone would like to become his pen friend. This seemed such an extraordinary request from an unknown correspondent in an unknown country (as China was, even to its neighbours, in the 1950s) that the letter was at first treated with considerable suspicion. Eventually, after checking with the regional headquarters of the communist party, the headmaster pinned up a translation of the letter on the notice board, asking if anyone would like to reply to it. Nursultan Nazarbayev was the only one of Kaskelen School's 250 pupils to take up this offer, starting what became an exchange of several letters with his Beijing pen friend. When asked why he was bothering to do this, he told the deputy headmaster 'Because I am interested in learning about China'.

Nazarbayev's early curiosity gave him wider horizons than his contemporaries. He was also blessed with deeper family roots than were usual in the rootless local community of newly arrived immigrants. For although he had been raised in hardscrabble poverty, he took immense pride in his Kazakh ancestry. He felt secure in his home environment, honouring his parents Abish and Aljan with a love that was warmly reciprocated. So, as he came towards the end of his schooldays in the summer of 1958, eighteen year old Nursultan was a well rounded young man with academic abilities that he knew were good enough to win him a place at one of the Soviet Union's best universities. 'In my last months before graduating from high school I had more or less decided to become a scientist specialising in chemistry' he has recalled. 'That was partly because I was good at science and partly because I had been impressed by the speeches of the new Soviet leader, Nikita Khrushchev, who often made broadcasts about the importance of chemistry in raising the productivity of agriculture. So that is what I planned to study at a top university in Moscow.'

*　　*　　*

(III) THE RISE TO THE LEADERSHIP

The plan for a university education never materialized. Although Nazarbayev had the grades for it, he was attracted by other ambitions. A giant new steel plant was being built by the Soviet Ministry of Industry in Temirtau, a town only 300 miles from Chemolgan in the province of Karaganda. Training courses in the Temirtau Technical School were offered to members of *Komsomol*, the young communist league, who were willing to study metallurgy in preparation for becoming steel-workers. Attracted by the advertised promise of 'the highest wages', a few weeks after his eighteenth birthday Nazarbayev applied for a job at Temirtau by presenting himself at the *Komsomol* headquarters in Stalin Avenue, Almaty. The manager on duty, Sabit Zhadanov, was impressed by the bright young village boy and urged him to study at university rather than training for the manual labour of a metallurgist. 'But Nazarbayev was very stubborn,' recalled Zhadanov. He quoted one of the mottos of *Komsomol* which was, 'If you are a member of *Komsomol* you will be the first to face the challenges of the front line and the last to take the bonuses and privileges of the easy life'.

Although Nazarbayev could spout the right phrases from Moscow's handbook of *Komsomol* doctrine, he was at heart much more of a nationalist than a communist. Self promotion was his *credo*, and in that spirit he managed to get himself elected to party membership by one of the 'shops' or groups of workers at the steelworks. 'I was an ambitious young man and party membership was the route to advancement', he later recalled. 'If I had thought it would have helped my ambition in those days to be a Buddhist I would have become a Buddhist. But as it was I became a member of the Communist Party – and a good one'.

In fact Nazarbayev received mixed reviews from his elders and betters in the party hierarchy. Because he was both articulate and photogenic he became something of a *Komsomol* pin-up boy, memorably pictured in *Pravda* as a typical Temirtau steelworker and invited to travel to international youth festivals as a debater.

But his capacity to argue also got him into trouble. He was nearly expelled from the party for breaches of discipline. When he was First Secretary of the Communist Party Committee of the steel mills at Temirtau he openly criticized the incompetent management of the steelworks and leaked his views to a journalist. This manoeuvre was a high risk strategy. In December 1972 Nazarbayev was summoned to Moscow to attend hearings by the Central Committee. But on the eve of the hearings the legendary Politburo chief Mikhail Suslov had a private meeting with the trouble making young whistle blower and encouraged him to make even more trouble at the plenary session of the committee.

Under Suslov's protection Nazarbayev not only survived but prospered. He was given responsibility for rebuilding the infrastructure in and around the Temirtau steelworks, doing the job so well that at thirty-five he was appointed regional party committee secretary for industry in the province of Karaganda. Three years later, in 1979, he was promoted to the secretariat of the Kazakh Communist Party as the Secretary responsible for economy and industry. This changed his political status from a regional to a national figure. At thirty-nine he had become a member of the principal governing body of the Soviet Republic of Kazakhstan.

For the next seven years of his career Nazarbayev was at first a favourite son and then a feuding rival of Dinmukhamed Kunayev, the most important politician in Kazakhstan whose friendship with Leonid Brezhnev had resulted in his appointment to the Soviet Politburo. Like First Secretary Kunayev, Nazarbayev was fluent in Russian and skilful at courting the party *apparatchiks* in Moscow. But there was an important difference between the two outstanding Kazakh political leaders of their respective generations. While Kunayev was Moscow's man first and a Kazakh second, Nazarbayev was privately sceptical of the Moscow bureaucracy and openly proud of his Kazakh roots and culture.

In 1984, when his relationship with Kunayev was still working smoothly Nazarbayev became Prime Minister of Kazakhstan. At forty-four he was the youngest Prime Minister in all the republics of the Soviet Union. When Mikhail Gorbachev became Soviet leader, he saw Nazarbayev as a kindred spirit and supporter of the new policies of *glasnost* (openness) and *Perestroika* (reconstruction) and for a short period Nazarbayev was named to the powerful Moscow Politburo.

Back in Kazakhstan there were growing tensions in the relationship with Kunayev who subjected his former protégé to an uncomfortable KGB investigation. Nazarbayev riposted by making an extraordinary attack on Kunayev in a speech to the Party Congress of Kazakhstan in

February 1986. This was more than a clash of personalities. Nazarbayev was outraged by the failure, waste, stagnation and corruption of the First Secretary's enfeebled regime. His open revolt fuelled further criticism within Kazakhstan making it increasingly clear that Kunayev's days were numbered. The ageing First Secretary resigned in December 1986 but his parting shot was to block Nazarbayev from the top job. 'I advise you to send a good Russian strongman to lead Kazakhstan', was Kunayev's valedictory recommendation to Gorbachev, who said with the wisdom of hindsight some years later: 'We fell into the trap that the old fox had set for us. And we made a big mistake'.

Gorbachev's big mistake in not selecting Nazarbayev for the vacant post of First Secretary of Kazakhstan in 1986 was to have historic consequences. This was because the news of Gennady Kolbin's appointment to the post unleashed an unexpected wave of protest on the grounds he was a Russian. The intelligentsia of the republic had felt assured that their new leader, like the departing Kunayev, would be a Kazakh. Kolbin was seen as a throwback to the old 'Moscow knows best' mindset of Soviet autocracy. In anger, students, teachers and many others took to the streets. Their demonstrations proved to be the first manifestation of the nationalities problem which came to haunt and eventually to destroy the Soviet Union.

The demonstrations that began in Almaty on 16 December 1986, later known as *Jeltoqsan,* took everyone by surprise including Nazarbayev. He had accepted Kolbin's appointment so he was astonished to be told that several hundred young people were marching towards the government buildings in Brezhnev Square to protest against their new Russian leader.

Political demonstrations were unprecedented in Kazakhstan. Nazarbayev was privately sympathetic to the students, particularly since their protest was a peaceful one consisting of nothing much more sinister than holding aloft banners with slogans such as *We want a Kazakh leader, Give us a Leninist nationalities policy. Every nation needs its own national leader.*

Publicly, however, Nazarbayev remained loyal to the regime. He came down to Brezhnev Square to urge restraint to the marchers. 'His main concern was to warn us that we could easily get hurt', recalled the student leader Nurtai Sabilyenov, 'He kept saying, don't let this get out of hand. I will report your views but be patient. Moscow always chooses the leader and they are not going to change their minds'. After leaving the demonstrators Nazarbayev went back into the government building and advised his new boss, Gennady Kolbin, to be cautious. His recommendation was that officials should mingle with the crowds and engage in a dialogue with them.

Nazarbayev's advice for dialogue was ignored. Senior Kremlin security officials arrived from Moscow to impose their *diktat* on the situation. They decided to fly in the Special Forces *Spetznaz* troops from bases all over the Soviet Union. On the morning of 18 December when some 15,000 young demonstrators were parading around the city centre, the *Spetznaz* launched a brutal counter attack on them, code named *Operation Snowstorm*.

Nazarbayev, although Prime Minister of Kazakhstan, was kept in the dark about *Operation Snowstorm*. So he had to watch it from the sidelines with growing horror. The students were doing nothing more provocative than waving their banners and singing patriotic Kazakh folk songs, particularly *Elimai* whose lyrics recount the courage of seventeenth century nomads resisting Jungar invaders. Twentieth century courage was required as police and troops arrested 8,000 of the demonstrators, using violence that resulted in two deaths and over 200 serious injuries. For the next twelve hours the authorities used ruthless tactics. They included beating and stripping many of the students before dumping them, half naked, on the outskirts of the city into the bitterly cold December night. These moves resulted in the short term suppression of the *Jeltoqsan* protest. But in the longer term a private legacy of bitterness spread through Kazakhstan and far beyond it. This was to have profound consequences throughout the Soviet Union over the next four years as other more determined nationalistic movements followed the example of the Almaty demonstrators and took to the streets in their own rebellions against centralized rule from Moscow.

Nazarbayev's reputation rose in the aftermath of *Jeltoqsan*. He was still the No 2 man in the government of the Soviet Republic of Kazakhstan but the No 1 man was reviled as a Moscow puppet. First Secretary Kolbin accelerated the twilight of Soviet authority. In appearance he was a caricature of a Russian *apparatchik* – thick set, red-faced, heavy drinking and administratively incompetent. His attempts to purge Kazakhstan's universities of the professors who had taught the student demonstrators of *Jeltoqsan* further exacerbated the tensions between Soviet *dirigisme* and local nationalism. This was a problem that was also erupting in other parts of the crumbling Soviet empire. There was growing unrest in the Baltic States, in Georgia, in Ukraine and even in Moscow itself where *Pamyat*, a Russian nationalist group linked to Boris Yeltsin, organized huge anti-Kremlin demonstrations.

Responding to these pressures, Mikhail Gorbachev announced a reformist agenda in his 1989 book *Perestroika: New Thinking for our Country and The World*. His plans to give reconstruction and greater autonomy to the republics were a case of too little, too late. At least he realized that Kazakhstan, where the nationalities demonstrations began, needed a fresh start. So Kolbin was moved back to Moscow creating a vacancy for the post of First Secretary. As Gorbachev described the situation to this author:

'We had to fix the error we had made with Kolbin. That was our first big mistake in inter-ethnic relations and I was determined not to repeat it. We had all come to accept that Kazakhs should run their own republic, and we gave them the right to decide who should be their new leader.'

Kazakhstan was allowed to carry out a surprisingly democratic consultation process at all levels of society before the new First Secretary was chosen. Soundings were taken among municipal organizations, opinion formers in the intelligentsia, workers groups from various industries and even among ordinary citizens on street corners. Only after these efforts to test public opinion had been made was the Central Committee of the Communist Party of Kazakhstan convened to decide on the choice of its First Secretary. New ground was broken here too. For the Central Committee took the surprising

66

step of organising a free vote in a secret ballot. It was the first time in the history of any Soviet republic that such a democratic process had ever taken place. This election was held on 1 June 1989. By an overwhelming majority and with the support of many of his former opponents, Nursultan Nazarbayev won the vote and became the new leader of Kazakhstan.

* * *

(IV) THE ANTI-NUCLEAR PRESIDENT

Nazarbayev learned a great deal from *Jeltoqsan* and its aftermath. Having risen to power through the communist system he was no natural democrat. Yet he understood that his fellow Kazakhs were developing a taste for expressing their feelings in democratic ways. So he explored this new tendency in two intriguing moves.

First, he tacitly encouraged a new wave of *Jeltoqsan* demonstrating which took place in Almaty in February 1990. This time the protestors were demanding the pardon and full rehabilitation of those who had been jailed or dismissed from their jobs following the original 1986 upheavals in Brezhnev Square. Nazarbayev backed these demands and issued a decree formally rehabilitating those who had been prosecuted or disciplined for their participation in *Jeltoqsan*. He also made 17 December the annual commemoration day of those events, naming it *Day of Democratic Renewal for the Republic of Kazakhstan*.

The second Nazarbayev exploitation of the unaccustomed processes of democracy involved a challenge to the Soviet Union's use of the Semipalatinsk region of Kazakhstan as a testing ground for nuclear weapons. Controlled explosions had taken place at this site since 1949 at the rate of one every three weeks. But the rigid secrecy surrounding the nuclear program had been so ruthlessly enforced by the Soviet military that ordinary Kazakhs did not dare to discuss it openly among themselves even when the effects of radiation were casting a terrible blight over the health of the population.

In 1986 the nuclear disaster at Chernobyl in the Ukraine raised the threshold of fear among the people of Semipalatinsk that a comparable catastrophe might one day befall them. These anxieties increased in 1989 when an underground explosion at the polygon testing centre caused a serious leak of radiation across the region. Demonstrations against the tests took place outside the House of Writers in Almaty organized by the well known poet Olzhas Suleimenov. This was the beginning of the *Semei-Nevada* movement which drew massive support across the whole spectrum of Kazakh society. Nazarbayev gave at first clandestine and later open support, to this growing wave of anti-nuclear protest. He encouraged Olzhas Suleimenov to stand as a candidate for the Supreme Soviet Parliament in a vacant seat in the Semipalatinsk district. Thanks to Nazarbayev's influence behind the scenes Suleimenov won both the nomination and the election, thus giving the anti-nuclear cause a popular platform.

Although the Soviet military were furious about these manifestations of open hostility within Kazakhstan to their testing activities at Semipalatinsk, they backed down and cancelled a planned expansion of the site. This reversal was caused by the political atmosphere of unrest across the Soviet Union in 1989–90. The conjunction of political crises, economic crises and bloody ethnic clashes accelerated the slide towards chaos. 'The most turbulent year was 1990 when it sometimes seemed as if the whole Union was ablaze', recalled Nazarbayev. He himself became a beneficiary of that turbulence when as part of a more general decentralisation of power to the republics he was elevated by the Kremlin to the rank of President of the Soviet Republic of Kazakhstan on 22 April 1990.

If Gorbachev and others responsible for Nazarbayev's promotion thought they were appointing a compliant leader who would govern the republic in accordance with Moscow's priorities, they soon found that they had made a big mistake. For Nazarbayev was now marching to the drumbeat of democratic pressure, in step with the wave of popular feeling that were becoming so apparent.

Less than a month after assuming his new title of President,

Nazarbayev launched an initiative that shook the military establishment of Moscow to the core of its nuclear being. This was the
holding of an international conference in Almaty in May 1990 with
the title *Electors of Peace Against Nuclear Arms*. It brought together
anti-nuclear campaigners from all parts of Kazakhstan and from
thirty countries around the world. The climax of the conference
was a peace march in Almaty followed by similar mass demonstrations in Semipalatinsk and Karaganda. The latter protest rally was
magnified by over 130,000 miners marching from the Karaganda
coalfields.

In a fit of angry reaction to these events, the Soviet military high
command announced that three further nuclear tests would take
place on the Semipalatinsk site in the autumn of 1991. But by now,
Nazarbayev had discovered that the power of popular protest in
Kazakhstan was far greater than the power of official announcements
by the Kremlin. In a defiant move that made him a hero at home and
a hate figure to the military in Moscow he issued a Presidential decree
banning all nuclear testing in Semipalatinsk. On the same day as this
decree was published in Almaty the Soviet defence ministry made a face
saving announcement in Moscow saying that the three nuclear explosions scheduled to take place in Semipalatinsk would be moved to the
Arctic test site of Novaya Zemlya.

This marked the end of Kazakhstan's forty year long nightmare
of nuclear testing. It was also the beginning of Nazarbayev's understanding of the power of democracy. As he himself has written:

In those days we learned about democracy. It was one of the first independent steps of
an independent Kazakhstan. We recognized and began correcting the mistakes of the
totalitarian Soviet past. We set forth on a new democratic path. And the foundation of
that path was laid in that historic decision for a non-nuclear Kazakhstan.

* * *

(IV) THE SURPRISING SURVIVOR

As Nazarbayev's fine words about Kazakhstan's 'new democratic path' imply, he appeared at the time when he spoke them to be committed to progress along this road. This is not a view of him shared by many western commentators. They have been quick to label him with unflattering and undemocratic epithets such as 'dictator'; 'autocrat'; or 'repressive ruler'. Whose perception is right?

In attempting to answer this question, it is worth examining the tensions between the young Nazarbayev on his rise to power and the older Nazarbayev firmly established in power.

In his youth Nazarbayev was a rebel in the cause of progress away from the sclerotic and centralized bureaucracy of the Soviet system. He hated the suppression of the Kazakh identity and of its heritage, history, culture and language. There were times when he showed spirited resistance to the pressures applied to him by party *apparatchiks*. Those pressures included two major KGB investigations, disciplinary procedures against him for being disloyal or disobedient and some unpleasant personal harassment. All this was part of a bigger picture. On the one hand Nazarbayev was a pragmatic can-do solver of problems, going along with the system in order to get along in his career. But at the same time he drew independent strength from his Kazakh roots and his rapport with ordinary workers in the mines and the steel plant. He was never an insider of the communist officials club. He was always an outsider who thought and spoke for himself.

The side of the young Nazarbayev which liked to speak out critically and which chafed against the abuses of autocratic power was greatly encouraged by the two manifestations of democratic protest – *Jeltoqsan* and *Semei-Nevada* which changed Kazakhstan's history. But having ridden the tigers of these movements when the Soviet Union was falling apart, Nazarbayev did not immediately know how to handle them when Kazakhstan was standing alone.

In some ways it was surprising that Nazarbayev did not leap on board the democracy bandwagon that was starting to roll or perhaps lurch forward in the Russian speaking world of the 1990s. He could easily have initiated some of the first democratic moves, enthusiastically applauded in the West, which were made by Gorbachev, Yeltsin and a regiment of other reformers in the Moscow firmament of post communist power brokers. But although Nazarbayev had a more stable base of support in his home country, and better credentials as a beneficiary of domestic democracy movements than his Russian counterparts, he was more cautious. As chaos confronted every republic in the crumbling Soviet Union, Nazarbayev put the politics of survival ahead of the politics of democratic experiment. As a result the western media promptly pigeon holed him into the stereotypes mentioned earlier, particularly 'dictator' and 'autocrat'. With the wisdom of hindsight it might have been better to describe him as 'the surprising survivor'.

Most observers gave Kazakhstan only a slim chance of surviving for more than a decade as a national state. It had no agreed borders with its mega-neighbours China or Russia. Both seemed predatory, Moscow aggressively so. The Kremlin behaved particularly badly by causing currency upheavals, oil pipeline robberies, trade obstructions and an inflation crisis. But gradually Nazarbayev steered through these troubled waters. He created the Tenge as Kazakhstan's sovereign currency. He devised a national constitution. After heroic efforts of personal diplomacy with the Russian President Boris Yeltsin, Nazarbayev established a secure northern frontier and a deal that gave Kazakhstan a favourable share of the Caspian Sea's oil riches. The economy started to grow as the first foreign investors arrived and oil production increased. Relations with China improved. Thanks again to a personal diplomatic relationship Nazarbayev created this time with PRC Chairman Jiang Zemin, the two countries signed and ratified an historic border agreement.

Although Kazakhstan slowly stabilized, a sinister shadow was created by the country's greatest problem. Nazarbayev eventually turned it into the opportunity to put his country's relationship with the West on to a favourable footing. This was the problem of Kazakhstan's nuclear weapons. Solving it was the President's finest hour. Understanding what was achieved on this issue is crucial to Kazakhstan's past, present and future.

5

Nuclear Past, Nuclear Future

(I) WASHINGTON'S POSTER BOY

In the rarefied circles of international experts on weapons of mass destruction, Nursultan Nazarbayev has iconic status. The respect for him comes from the actions he took in the turbulent years after the break up of the Soviet Union to renounce control of the 1200 nuclear missiles stationed within his borders and to make his country a nuclear free nation. Those were the main reasons why in April 2010 Kazakhstan and its President were feted at a global nuclear security summit in Washington DC attended by forty-seven nations. President Barack Obama was fulsome in his tributes. 'You are one of the model leaders of the world', he said in his speech of welcome to Nursultan Nazarbayev, 'we could not have this summit without your presence'.

The impression that the President of Kazakhstan was the star of the show increased during the week of televised events and diplomatic dealings. A sudden and unexpected foreign policy drama – a violent coup in Kyrgyzstan – also propelled Nazarbayev to centre stage. For he, President Obama and President Medvedev of Russia negotiated a temporary solution to the crisis which involved giving sanctuary in Kazakhstan to the ousted Kyrgyz leader, Kurmanbek Bakiyev.

Nazarbayev's pivotal role, well reported live on all TV channels, was that of the deal broker between two mutually suspicious great powers each of whom was concerned about the threat to their respective military bases in Kyrgyzstan. To the uninitiated American viewing audience, which probably had difficulty in distinguishing Kyrgyzstan from Kazakhstan, Nazarbayev emerged as one of the good guys.

This status was enhanced by Kazakhstan's carefully timed announcement that it would grant new overflying rights for US troops and weapons to Afghanistan. Washington had long been negotiating for what the Pentagon called the Northern Distribution Network as it reduced the flying time between the US and Kabul to little over twelve hours. The Chief of the White House Staff, Rahm Emanuel, thanked Nazarbayev for bringing such a welcome 'house gift'.

There were other smaller diplomatic indications that Nazarbayev was being treated as top dog of the summit. He stayed at the Presidential Suite at the Willard Hotel – a far more spacious set of rooms than those occupied by France's President Sarkozy and other heads of government staying there.

On the second day of the conference, Nazarbayev was presented with the East-West Peace and Preventive Diplomacy Award at a glittering dinner in his honour attended by many Washington notables including the President's National Security Adviser, General James Jones and former Secretary of State Madeleine Albright. 'I expect you are going to talk about democracy Madeleine' said Nazarbayev in his playful acceptance speech, 'as you do every time we meet'. To the chagrin of the human rights lobby, this insouciance towards the progress of democracy in Kazakhstan continued all week. Even President Obama handled the subject helpfully by welcoming his guest from the Steppes with the emollient words: 'We too are working to improve our democracy ... You don't ever reach democracy, you have to keep working on it'.

The impression that Nazarbayev had literally become the administration's poster boy was heightened by a huge photograph of him displayed on advertising hoardings all over the city and at every central Washington bus stop. Beneath a picture of the President the caption explained that Kazakhstan had given up the nuclear missiles it inherited from the Soviet Union because atomic testing had sickened 1.5 million of its people. 'That's why we got rid of our nuclear arsenal, the world's fourth largest. And that is why we call on the world to follow example. There is no other way to build a safer world' the poster quoted Nazarbayev.

Nazarbayev's record as the leader of the first nation on the planet to voluntarily renounce the possession and use of nuclear weapons gave him an aura of saintliness at the summit. There were times during the conference tributes to him that a halo almost seemed to be hovering above his head! But however much he enjoyed the compliments, Nazarbayev was moving to a fresh strategic agenda of nuclear objectives.

First he consolidated his reputation for responsible nuclear security co-operation by agreeing to close, in co-operation with the United States Government, Kazakhstan's surviving BN-350 plutonium production reactor.

After announcing that his country had become the world's largest uranium producer, Nazarbayev then put down some important markers outlining Kazakhstan's plans to manufacture uranium pellets and rods on the massive scale required to meet the soaring world demand for nuclear power in the new generation of power stations under construction or being designed.

The scale of this vision surprised the assembled summit delegates, not least because of the political U-turn it required. The paradox here was that a country which had suffered from some of the worst nuclear outrages of the twentieth century was now aiming to become one of the largest developers of peaceful nuclear power in the twenty-first century. This turnaround story could well be headlined 'From horrors to riches'.

* * *

(II) TELLING THE HORROR STORY

Kazakhstan's nuclear history was a saga of tragedy. The disasters started in the late 1940s when military commanders in Moscow took the strategic decision to designate the region around Semipalatinsk in the north east of the then Soviet Republic of Kazakhstan as the principal testing ground for nuclear weapons. The first atmospheric nuclear test on the Semipalatinsk site (a land area approximately the size of Wales) was conducted by the Soviet Army in 1949. Over the next forty years, throughout the nuclear arms race of the Cold War era, Kazakhstan became the Soviet Union's weapons laboratory.

Between 1949 and 1989 tests took place at the rate of one every three weeks. There were 752 explosions, 78 at ground level, 26 in the atmosphere and the remainder underground. The regularity and radioactivity of these tests, carried out with virtually no safety precautions for the local people, had devastating consequences for the national environment and for the health of the population.

Within a few years of the early thermonuclear explosions, some of them twenty times greater than the Hiroshima bomb, stories spread across the Steppes about the horrific consequences for animal and human life. The Kazakhs, who made up ninety-nine per cent of the ethnic population around Semipalatinsk, were appalled. Their national anger was aroused partly because it was the nomadic people of the region who suffered the worst effects of radiation such as stillbirths, deformities, cancer and mental illness; partly because the district of Semipalatinsk was venerated with an almost sacred status in Kazakh culture as the birthplace of their greatest poet, Abay; and partly because the Kazakh tribes felt a natural if not mystical bond between man and land which was suddenly being violated by the perverted science of nuclear testing.

Because of the ruthless imposition of military secrecy on the testing activities at Semipalatinsk, no-one in Kazakhstan had a clear picture of the nature and extent of the nuclear program. But despite the threat of capital punishment some Kazakhs did talk about the horrors that were occurring. As a young man Nursultan Nazarbayev began working in 1959 as a steelworker in Temirtau, some two hundred miles from the nuclear testing grounds. He became accustomed to the flashes in the sky, the mushroom clouds, and the earth tremors that were part and parcel of the Soviet experiments. Moreover, a fellow steelworker and metallurgy student, Tuleutai Suleymenov, became a close friend who revealed much more detailed information about the effects of the tests to Nazarbayev.

Tuleutai Suleymenov came from a family who lived at the foothills of Degelen, a mountain in the heart of the Semipalatinsk testing area. When Suleymenov was thirteen his father died of brain cancer; his elder sister died of leukaemia two years later; his second sister was mentally retarded; and his third sister suffered throughout her life from radiation sores on her forehead. The agonies of the Suleymenov family made a deep impact on Nazarbayev who used them as a graphic example of the personal agonies his countrymen were forced to endure when he came to conduct international disarmament negotiations some 30 years later.

*   *   *

(III) UNILATERAL NUCLEAR DISARMAMENT

Like all his compatriots, Nazarbayev knew little or nothing about the details of the nuclear program that Moscow's military commanders had been implementing for over four decades in Kazakhstan. But in the dying months of the Soviet Union he managed to impose a ban against testing any nuclear devices on his country's territory. This move, although it appalled the Soviet military, was wildly popular domestically for there had been a series of mass demonstrations against the tests in Kazakh cities. Nazarbayev later called these protests 'one of our first lessons in democracy'.

When the USSR finally collapsed in December 1991, Nazarbayev as President of the newly independent nation was officially briefed about the full extent of the weapons of mass destruction stationed on Kazakhstan's territory. 'The information I was given was new to me' he has recalled. 'It had previously been a tightly-held secret known only to the highest officers of the Red Army'. The secret revelations staggered Nazarbayev. He learned that in terms of fire power, Kazakhstan was the custodian of over 1,200 nuclear warheads for Intercontinental Ballistic Missiles (ICBMs). This arsenal consisted of 104 SS18 ICBMs, each equipped with ten MIRV warheads (multiple independently targeted re-entry vehicles) with a range of around 12,000 kilometres. The missiles were stationed in 148 launch silos located across the country, with the largest concentrations in Akmolinsk, Kyzylorda and Semipalatinsk. They were under the control of the Soviet army's Strategic Rocket Command (RVSN), the highest military elite of the former USSR. In addition, Kazakhstan was the base of the Soviet's 79th Air Division, whose fleet of forty Bear H6 and H16 aircraft were armed with long range bombs and missiles. The totality of these forces and weapons gave

Kazakhstan the fourth largest concentration of nuclear weapons in the world after the United States, Russia and the former Soviet bases in Ukraine. In comparison, the number of warheads controlled by Britain (296), France (512) and China (284) combined were smaller in number than those located in Kazakhstan.

Nazarbayev now found himself President of a country that had suddenly inherited a formidable and terrifying assembly of nuclear weapons. When he inspected the bases and missile launch sites (particularly the Akmolinsk silos containing the huge SS18 ICBMs, known in the West as 'Satans'), he was filled with foreboding:

'There was something truly satanic about the fierce array of ballistic missiles with separating nuclear warheads based on our territory' recalled Nazarbayev. 'They were overwhelming just in their size. I always felt uncomfortable simply looking at the enormous body of "Satans" – thirty-four metres tall and three metres in diameter. By their very existence, these missiles aroused a feeling in me of dread and horror. I had a sense that they could turn against their owners at any moment with satanic unpredictability.'

As the chief 'new owner' of Kazakhstan's nuclear weapons, Nazarbayev was not short of advice on what to do with them. His fellow countrymen, although united in their opposition to nuclear testing, were surprisingly divided on the right national policy for the weapons themselves. There were hawks who wanted to maintain a permanent nuclear strike force under Kazakhstani control as a deterrent to potential aggressors from violating the security of the country's borders. There were bargainers who advocated retaining the warheads for some years until they could be exchanged for security guarantees of Kazakhstan's sovereignty from the world's nuclear powers. And there were doves who demanded immediate, unilateral and total nuclear disarmament. As Nazarbayev listened to these discordant voices, he sometimes quoted an old Kazakh proverb: 'Take you in? But you're a monster! Chase you away? But you're a treasure.' It was his way of admitting that the issue of what to do with the country's nuclear weapons was a complex one which would best be resolved by careful negotiations and, if possible, with support from a national consensus. As Nazarbayev put it: 'We had no choice but to embark on the difficult path of measuring conclusions and counter-arguments, doubts and fears, in a grand debate as we deliberated whether or not Kazakhstan would become a nuclear power'.

The outcome of this 'grand debate' was almost inevitable unless Kazakhstan wanted to become a pariah nation or rogue state on the level of North Korea. As this was the last outcome Nazarbayev wanted, he quickly entered into disarmament negotiations with the US Secretary of State James Baker. Some of their initial discussions took place in the *Banya* or steam bath of Nazarbayev's home in Almaty giving rise to the label 'sauna diplomacy'. However the political temperature of the negotiations never became over heated. James Baker found Nazarbayev 'extremely intelligent and capable', and had no serious difficulties in striking a deal with him.

Although the principles of Kazakhstan's commitment to nuclear disarmament were established early, the practicalities, technicalities and international agreements took time. There were visits by Nazarbayev to Presidents George H. W. Bush and Bill Clinton in Washington. Vice President Al Gore and Secretary of State Warren Christopher came to Almaty. So did US Senators Sam Nunn and Richard Lugar whose Nunn-Lugar Program assigned over US$400 million of Congressional Funding to pay for the physical movement of Kazakhstan's missiles out of their 40 metre silos and to compensate the country for the value of the enriched uranium in its 1,200 warheads.

Meanwhile President Yeltsin and the government of Russia had to be kept on side as the former military might of the Soviet Union was decommissioned and dispersed. 'This was not a mere matter of politeness' recalled Nazarbayev. 'I needed to understand President Yeltsin's position. The whereabouts of the missiles on the territories of our two republics was something the two of us should decide together.'

Throughout the complexities of the protracted international negotiations, Nazarbayev impressed his interlocutors from America, Russia and from the International Atomic Energy Agency (IAEA), with his mastery of the nuclear detail. But eventually all the major objectives were accomplished. Kazakhstan signed and ratified the Nuclear

Non-Proliferation Treaty. The missiles were moved or destroyed and their warheads made safe. Kazakhstan's nuclear history was a successfully and peacefully closed chapter. But there were still some surprises to come.

* * *

(IV) THE NOT-SO-EASY CLEAN UP

As part of the removal operations for the Soviet missiles the International Atomic Energy Agency carried out an inventory in 1994 to check whether there was any other nuclear material located in Kazakhstan.

This inventory produced two extraordinary discoveries, both of which appeared to have been 'forgotten' by the Soviet Union. The first was a store of highly enriched uranium at Ulba Metallurgical Plant near the city of Ust-Kamenogorsk in eastern Kazakhstan. The second was an undetonated charge of radioactive plutonium buried in a deep shaft at Semipalatinsk. Both required the personal involvement of Nazarbayev.

The inventory taken by the nuclear weapons inspectorate with the help of Kazakhstani experts showed that at a nuclear waste processing plant at Ulba, there was a previously unknown storage depot containing 600 kilograms of highly enriched weapons-grade uranium. This was enough explosive material to make at least 20 nuclear warheads. Nazarbayev immediately reported the discovery to the military authorities responsible for nuclear matters in Moscow. He was amazed by their dismissive response, which was in effect to profess complete ignorance of this lethal store of uranium and to say, in effect, 'It's all yours'.

'The Russians must have known all about this material' recalled Nazarbayev. 'After all, the Soviet Union used to be one country, and all the records of nuclear stores must have been held in one place, presumably Moscow. At first I believed that these supplies of weapons-grade uranium were part of the Soviet military's secret plans for a war against China in the 1960s. They built underground bases all over Eastern Kazakhstan for this purpose. But whatever the original objectives were, I eventually concluded that the military had simply lost the records and forgotten about the store of weapons-grade uranium at Ulba. They made it clear that it was all ours, and that we were free to dispose of it ourselves.'

Knowing that Kazakhstan did not have the technical resources to carry out such a disposal of weapons-grade uranium, Nazarbayev sent a message through diplomatic channels to Washington. This resulted in an urgent visit to Almaty by the US Defense Secretary William J. Perry, who later claimed credit for preventing 'what might have been history's biggest and most devastating case of loose nukes'. This was more a case of loose talk by Perry, for there had never been any 'nukes', and the uranium depot had always been held under strict security conditions. However, there were rumours, picked up by the eavesdroppers of the CIA and NSA, that an Iranian terrorist group had learned of the Ulba cache of weapons-grade uranium and were discussing among themselves how to get their hands on it. This fragment of intelligence, flimsy though it was, precipitated a mood of alarm among security analysts in Washington. In theory, their concern was justified because if just a few kilograms of this weapons-grade uranium had been acquired by terrorists, the consequences could have been devastating. To give one example: If Al Qaeda had used one percent or six kilos of the Ulba Uranium in its attack on the World Trade Center, then most of lower Manhattan would have been reduced to rubble.

In practice, however, there was no likelihood of any such potential catastrophe, because Defence Secretary Perry and President Nazarbayev co-operated so well and so swiftly. Under their joint orders, *Operation Sapphire* took on the speed and spine-tingling drama of a spy movie. Once the American experts were admitted to the Ulba Metallurgical Plant inside the former Soviet 'closed city' of Ust-Kamenogorsk, they were able to trace the 'forgotten' 600 kilos of uranium back to a Soviet Navy programme of the 1970s intended to create a revolutionary new type of reactor for nuclear submarines. The reactor was designed to produce nuclear fuel rods which would enable Soviet subs to dive deeper, stay submerged longer and travel at a faster rate of knots than any submarine in the US Navy. The project became so costly that Soviet scientists nicknamed it 'Goldfish', because it would have been cheaper to have the submarines made of gold. Eventually, the reactor failed, the Goldfish never went to sea, the programme had to be abandoned and the weapons-grade uranium was transferred into a thousand steel canisters stored in the vaults of Ulba where it stayed, safe but forgotten, for over twenty years.

Nazarbayev was probably the first political leader since Leonid Brezhnev to learn about this project. There was no hesitation from the President of Kazakhstan in deciding what to do about this lethal store of 90 per cent enriched uranium. He sold it at the going rate for enriched uranium to the Americans (approximately US\$90 million), and handed over the responsibility to them of moving it back to the USA. So, on a weekend of November 1994, a fleet of C5 transport aircraft arrived in Almaty. Using a cover story that they were members of the International Atomic Energy Agency, thirty-one specialist US Navy personnel transferred the uranium to smaller nuclear canisters, loaded them aboard the C5s and flew the entire cargo back to a nuclear facility at Oak Ridge, Tennessee. Only after the last of the material arrived there did Secretary Perry announce the successful conclusion of Operation Sapphire at a Washington press conference on 25 November 1994. In a letter from the White House on that day, President Clinton told Nazarbayev: 'You deserve the world's praise ... This important operation reflects an expansion of trust in the maturing partnership between our two countries.'

There was one more domestic surprise on the nuclear front, which needed careful handling by Nazarbayev before the saga of the Semipalatinsk testing ground could be ended. This was the discovery of an undetonated 0.4 kiloton charge of plutonium buried 130 metres underground in shaft No 108-K. Nazarbayev called this hidden cache of radioactive explosive 'the forgotten stepchild of the test site'. It had been prepared for detonation by Soviet scientists under conditions of great secrecy in May 1991 as part of a planned test known as Experiment FO-100-SZLR. However, the political upheavals in the Soviet Union during the summer of 1991, including the abortive coup against Gorbachev, had caused the test to be delayed. Then Nazarbayev's Presidential Decree of 29 August 1991, banning all nuclear tests in Kazakhstan, turned the postponement into a prohibition. Thereafter, Semipalatinsk was officially dead as a nuclear test site, but it unexpectedly had a secret life of its own through this undetonated plutonium charge buried in shaft No 108-K.

Destroying this unexploded nuclear device deep underground was a highly complicated operation. Nazarbayev's first concern was whether it might explode spontaneously. He was not entirely convinced by the reassurances given to him by his experts, particularly when his principal adviser declared 'There is no danger' and then added in the next breath that there was the potential for an explosion if underground drillings near the shaft took place.

After considering various options, including the removal of the device and its transportation to Russia, Nazarbayev decided that the safest method of disposal would be to destroy it in its underground shaft by chemicals. So, on 31 May 1995, 400 kilograms of chemical explosives eliminated 'Object 108-K' – the 0.4 kiloton charge of radioactive plutonium. Nazarbayev regarded it as symbolic that the last nuclear device at the Semipalatinsk site was destroyed rather than exploded. 'That non-nuclear explosion symbolized Kazakhstan becoming a nuclear-free territory'.

Although the symbolism was real, the clean up of vulnerable nuclear material in the country remained incomplete until 2010. In the summer of that year a top secret operation was launched by the US-Kazakhstan joint energy partnership to shut down the BN-350 military plutonium reactor at Aktau which in Soviet times had been a military production base for nuclear warheads. Although no plutonium had been manufactured there for twenty years, the spent fuel it produced could still be militarily useful to a terrorist organization. So a secure facility to safeguard the plutonium was constructed in Semipalatinsk and the spent fuel was transported there.

'This was a massive high security operation', said the joint chairman of the US-Kazakh Energy Partnership Sauat Mynbaev, 'we carried it out with the help of US, UK and Kazakhstani nuclear experts. We had to transport the plutonium nearly 2,000 miles from Aktau to Semipalatinsk in 60 specially constructed rail containers. We did several rehearsals with each container protected by armed guards. It was successfully completed by the end of October 2010. As our joint announcement with the US government said:

"The completion of this program is one of the many highlights of the 15 year track record of strategic partnership and close cooperation between Kazakhstan and the United States in reducing nuclear threats in Kazakhstan".'

* * *

(V) KAZATOMPROM – THE EXPANSION OF URANIUM MINING AND NUCLEAR FUEL PRODUCTION

Although the threat of loose nukes has been eliminated, a new problem of loose money arrived in the early years of Kazatomprom. This was the umbrella organization set up by the state in 1997 to control uranium mining and nuclear fuel products for peaceful nuclear power stations.

Kazatomprom was headed in the first twelve years of its existence by a visionary and energetic Kazakh nuclear expert Mukhtar Dzhakishev. He transformed a virtually bankrupt collection of unexploited mining assets into the world's largest producer of uranium. Today Kazatomprom has an output of over 18,000 tons which gives it thirty per cent of the world market, way ahead of its nearest competitors Canada and Australia. This surge of production has coincided with a surge in world uranium prices to over \$68 per lb and a surge in present and prospective nuclear power generation which depends on fuel cycle products derived from raw uranium. Although the last of these surges is bound to be affected for a while in the aftermath of international reaction to the radiation crisis at Japan's Fukushima reactor, the long term prospects for the industry remain strong.

The world market in uranium products is complex involving refineries, processing plants, pelletisation factories, high technology centrifuges for fuel rods, fusion reactors and thermal reactors. There are huge investment requirements. As a result Kazakhstan has formed a number of joint ventures with Russia, France, China, Canada, Japan and the USA. World class companies are involved in these joint ventures such as Westinghouse, Toshiba, Rosatom TWEL and Uranium One.

With so much money and so many competing national interests involved in the expansion of global nuclear power it is unsurprising that political pressures and financial corruption can loom large in this secretive industry. Depending on whose story one is listening to, both ingredients have played their part in the recent upheavals at Kazatomprom.

On 21 May 2009 Mukhtar Dzakishev, the chief executive of Kazatomprom was arrested on charges of embezzlement and the illegal sale of assets to foreign companies. Much of the evidence against him at his trial involved his dealings with the Canadian led company Uranium One in which Kazatomprom held a strategic stake of thirty-five per cent in order to give it exclusive access to certain production and marketing rights. A secondary purpose of Kazatomprom's strategic stake was to prevent these production and marketing rights going to Russian interests. Inevitably the Russian interests were unhappy about the Dzakishev/Kazatomprom strategy and tried to undermine it by buying shares in Uranium One. Dzakishev in return tried to block the Russian shareholding by organising rival share purchases by Japanese and Chinese companies.

This tangled tale of corporate power struggles ended with the arrest of Dzakishev. There has been speculation that Dzakishev was a political victim rather than a criminal offender. As he himself put this argument in a tape smuggled out of his prison cell. 'The consequences of Mr Putin's visit to Kazakhstan 17–21 May were not good for me. Immediately after his visit I was taken into custody. It makes me think that this was a purely political decision'. Dzakishev was found guilty and sentenced to fourteen years imprisonment.

*   *   *

(VI) VLADIMIR SHKOLNIK

An interview with Vladimir Shkolnik is like an encounter with an express train whose driver – the new President of Kazatomprom – thunders forward on a mixture of optimism, ebullience and good humoured boastfulness.

'We expect to be the No 1 nuclear fuel company in the world', he says. 'The future for us is excellent because there is such huge global expansion of nuclear power, starting here in Asia. I have just come back from China which is now building twenty-six nuclear power stations with a further thirty-one approved. It plans to have 170 nuclear power stations altogether, but it produces only a small percentage of the fuel these facilities require. So China needs Kazakhstan's uranium.'

Asked if there is any danger that Kazakhstan could become too dependent on China for its export orders of uranium Vladimir Shkolnik answers:

'No, because the renaissance of nuclear power generation is a worldwide phenomenon. According to the strategic plans of industrialised countries over five hundred new nuclear power stations will be built in the next thirty years over and above the 434 plants that are now in operation, many of which will have to be rebuilt. Also the mission for Kazakhstan is not just to get raw uranium powder straight out of the mines. We are creating an industry here which will make enriched uranium pellets, uranium rods and assembling them into value added batteries which are called blocks. These can be exported for prices of $1 million per block'.

These optimistic forecasts were made some weeks before Japan's Fukushima nuclear reactor went into meltdown in March 2011. As a result China and some other countries have delayed or suspended parts of their future plans for nuclear power plants. But the probability is that, subject to some postponements and extra safety precautions, most programs will eventually go ahead. So Shkolnik remains a convinced believer, confident that Kazatomprom and its 25,000 employees are building an industrial empire which will one day be as important as oil and gas to the nation's economy.

This vision starts with the advantage that Kazakhstan has the world's largest deposits of uranium and can mine them at around $24 per lb.

This is a highly profitable extraction cost when the world uranium price is $68 per lb.

But there are two possible obstacles to the dream of making Kazakhstan an industrial centre of excellence for the nuclear power industry. The first is technology transfer and licensing requirements. Right now the country is only a vast uranium quarry for its customers. In order to enter the value added business, huge high tech plants have to be built under strict IAEA safeguards with all the appropriate licenses and permits. Shkolnik acknowledges the scale of the challenge but claims Kazatoprom will be manufacturing enriched uranium pellets by the end of 2011 with export licences already negotiated for Russia, China and Japan. However, this required setting up joint ventures with various international corporations who are at present carrying out parts of the enrichment process in their countries before the technology can be transferred to Kazakhstan's national enrichment plant at Ust-Kamenogorsk. This may take longer than some of the Kazatomprom optimists predict. But in the meantime the state owned company has plenty to do not only in uranium mining but also in developing its deposits of some of the rarest and most precious metals on the planet such as beryllium, tungsten, titanium, cadmium, all of which are in high demand in China, Korea, India and the western world.

Vladimir Shkolnik's grand master plan for making Kazatomprom the No 1 nuclear power generating company of the twenty-first century, has created some unease among those elements in the domestic population whose lives were so devastated by the nuclear blight of the Soviet era. The spectre of radiation leakages on the scale of another Chernobyl still haunt the imagination of older residents. When a correspondent from *The Guardian,* Tom Parfit, made a visit in December 2010 to the Semipalatinsk region which was and which again will be, the epicenter of nuclear activity in Kazakhstan he reported:

'As for ordinary Kazakhs, many are ambivalent about the nuclear renaissance which includes plans to store enriched fuel in the east of the country'.

'I'm against it', said a military officer in Semey. 'Please, no more dead fish in our rivers'.

Vladimir Shkolnik sounded rather defensive when asked about the degree of opposition to Kazatomprom's nuclear power expansion plans.

'We are a very socially orientated company. We build orphanages, homes and schools for those who have suffered', he said. 'In the areas of Southern Kazakhstan where we are developing our operations we are building roads and water supplies. This is all part of our public relations drive to make it clear that nuclear power is safe. My own experience of living and working in Kazakhstan for over 40 years is that if you are completely transparent and completely open with the public, the dialogue will convince them that we are protecting them. Of course, we have had many people and many NGOs who originally opposed our plans. But at the last public hearing we presented the radioactivity measurements taken not by Kazatomprom but by scientists from the NGOs. So everyone was convinced that the very low radiation levels around the uranium mines are well within the safety norms. Also people are reassured that we ship our raw uranium out to other countries who do the enrichment process at higher radiation levels. And of course the local people are pleased that so many jobs are created by Kazatomprom'.

The public relations debate on the safety of nuclear power is far from over. The tensions produced by the pro- and anti-arguments are bound to rise in the wake of the crisis in Japan caused by the meltdown in the Fukushima reactor. As a result Kazakhstan has new hurdles to overcome in its efforts to create a world-leading nuclear power industry from its natural resources. Yet as Kazatomprom already complies impeccably with the strictest IAEA safeguards there is no logical reason why the country would not be able to produce safe nuclear power even if the safeguards were made far stricter.

Logic, however, may not be the only driving force behind the decision-making process on nuclear power expansion. Emotion will play a strong part too, particularly in those parts of Kazakhstan where the horrific history of nuclear exploitation during the Soviet era still casts a long shadow. Kazatomprom will need to move ahead with special care towards its future development.

For it remains a strange paradox that the country that suffered some of the world's worst nuclear tragedies is now turning itself into a country which hopes to make the world's largest revenues from nuclear power. It will still require all the presentational skills of both the President of Kazatomprom and the President of Kazakhstan to reconcile the country's nuclear past with its nuclear future.

6

A Tale of Two Cities

(I) COMPLEMENTARY RIVALS

Kazatomprom's corporate headquarters are located in Almaty, as are most head offices of major businesses in the country including Kazakhmys, Eurasian Natural Resources Corporation (both FSTE 100 listed companies) and the national airline Air Astana. It is a reminder that for all the governmental activity that takes place in the brash new capital of Astana, the commercial and cultural centre of the nation is Almaty. A friendly rivalry exists between these two cities whose relationship can be compared to that of New York and Washington DC.

The comparison goes several steps further. Like the Big Apple Almaty is proud of its Opera House, its ballets, its museums, its cathedral and its stock exchange, its skyscrapers and its cosmopolitan market traders. Astana, like Washington DC, lives and breathes the business of government. It is home to all the ministries and departments or agencies of the state. Its White House, where the President and his key staff are located, is based on a rather grander model of 1600 Pennsylvania Avenue, one of over a hundred exotic public buildings.

For all its eye-catching architecture, Astana knows that it has a lot of catching up to do with its southern sister in the fields of cultural excellence and commercial vitality. Almaty has a slightly resentful enviousness of the political power and Presidential patronage that has so recently been bestowed on its northern rival. So this is a tale of two cities, who both complement and compete with each other as Kazakhstan's past history and future progress unfold in the changing tapestry of Central Asia in the twenty-first century.

*　*　*

(II) ALMATY'S ORIGINS AND LANDMARKS

The name Almaty translates as 'The place of the Apples' – a reference to the numerous fruit bearing orchards in and around the city whose eighteenth century arboriculturalists are said to have invented a special kind of apple by ingenious tree-grafting techniques. Named in Soviet days as Alma-Ata the nomadic and agricultural settlements of the area were transformed by Imperial Russia and then Soviet colonization into a trading centre combined with a regional capital. The first major turning point in this city's growth was its connection to the Turkestan and Trans-Siberian railway network in 1929. This led to commercial expansion, the influx of immigrants from all over Russia and Asia, and a visionary town plan which provided parks, botanical gardens and tree lined boulevards surrounded by imaginative architecture.

In the heyday of Soviet power Almaty was a major beneficiary of the rule of Dinmukhamed Kunayev, First Secretary of the Kazakhstan Communist Party 1959–86. He was a Kazakh national who rose to being the only Central Asian member of the Supreme Soviet Politburo. Kunayev's promotion owed much to his early friendship with Leonid Brezhnev who became the leader of the Soviet Union.

Kunayev's political connections enabled him to obtain funding for several monumental state buildings in Alma-Ata. They included the Palace of the Republic, the House of Friendship, the Kasteyev State Museum of Art, the Hotel Kazakhstan, the Academy of Science and the Kazakhfilm Studios and the Republic Palace of Schoolchildren and Pioneers. As the names of these edifices suggest they are examples of Soviet planning at its most solid and stately. Some were designed by the famous Moscow architect Alexey Shchusev who created a high level of interior and exterior design with neoclassical touches. The most attractive non-classical building in the city is the Abay Opera House whose Palladian columns and beautiful backdrop of the Alatau range of mountains make it one of Almaty's most iconic sights.

Other architectural gems are the Holy Ascension Cathedral, a multi-coloured wooden extravaganza of Imperial Russian Orthodox splendour and the charming Museum of Folk Musical Instruments designed by Andrei Zenkov. Both stand in Panfilov park whose huge military statues commemorate the valour of the Kazakh troops commanded by General Ivan Panfilov in the defence of Moscow against Hitler's armies in World War Two.

* * *

(III) THE COMMERCIAL CAPITAL

The architectural heritage of Alma-Ata's past glories is complemented by the glitz and glitter of the new commercial buildings in post-independence Almaty. The gloom of the communist era was followed by a capitalist boom in natural resources. Real estate prices shot up almost as high as the skyscrapers erected by mining companies like Kazakhmys.

The Chairman and Chief Executive of this corporation is the Korean born Vladimir Kim whose offices are an ostentatious oasis of opulence at the heart of the city. 'Money doesn't smell', he told me, 'we are confident that our output of copper is going up, that commodity prices are going up and that our share price will go up. But at the same time we know that our share price is strong because of our good relationship with the government. Without the direct support of the President we would not have launched this company on the London Stock Exchange with an IPO. At least eighty per cent of my staff did not feel comfortable with the IPO process but President Nazarbayev said to me, "Go and get access to the money of big international shareholders. This will bring transparency, confidence and new technology, not just to Kazakhmys but to the benefit of all Kazakhstan".'

One or two rungs on Almaty's commercial ladder below Vladimir Kim and his fellow mining tycoons and oligarchs are the rising gener-ation of younger entrepreneurs. I met a group of them in a fashionable Almaty Bar. They were the Kazakhstan chapter of the Young President's Organization (YPO), an international organization for successful young businessmen. To join the YPO anywhere in the world you have to be under forty-five, and the owner or CEO of a company with an annual sales turnover in excess of $US 10 million.

'We are all completely self made men', said Kazakhstan's YPO chairman, Nurlan Kapparov as he introduced his fellow chapter members, 'in this young country there has been no time to inherit wealth. And it is quite hard to make capital as an entrepreneur here because so much of our economy is still state regulated or foreign controlled. So we have to concentrate on the sectors that are deregulated'.

Between them the YPO members identified six parts of the economy in which small and medium sized enterprises (SMEs) were prospering because of deregulation. They were: Transportation; Food distribution; Tourism; Electrical Products and Retailing and Value added products in the oil and gas industries. But the Young President said that all these SME sectors combined represented only sixteen per cent of the economy while the remaining eighty-four per cent was controlled by large international corporations such as Chevron, Shell and British Gas; or by foreign investors; or by the government through its state holding company Samruk. Despite some genial grumbling about these constraints, the Harvard-educated Nurlan Kapparov and his fellow YPO members were bright, bullish and optimistic about the future prospects for their own companies. However, they struck a cautionary note about the future of entrepreneurship even in the nation's commercial capital:

'The number of entrepreneurs is not growing here in Almaty. Much the same people who started up their own businesses in 2000 are still setting the pace ten or twelve years later. The newcomers to the business scene are relatively few', said Erlan Sagadiev, the CEO of Frontier Mining, as other YPO heads nodded in agreement, 'the problem here is that too many young people dream of becoming a government official. There is still a dominant the-state-knows-best mentality here'.

*　*　*

(IV) THE ALMATY MENTALITY

'There is definitely an Almaty mentality because we are fiercely proud of our city and we love our way of life', says one government official, the Deputy Akim or Mayor of Almaty Serik Seidumanov, 'we are ten per cent of the population of the country with 1.5 million residents and we think of ourselves as well educated, well brought up, civilized and cultured.

'This is a city of beauty as you can see just by looking out of the window at our Tien-Shan mountains all around us and then by walking around our fine buildings, gardens and street water fountains.

'It is also a city of freedom with a fascinating history and we have been an international trading centre ever since the time when this was a staging post on the old silk road. So we think we are rather special.'

The enthusiasm of the Deputy Akim is largely justified. Almaty is as lively as it is beautiful. Its numerous street cafes and restaurants throb with both the latest hot music and the latest hot topics of discussion. When I was last there in January 2011 the controversy of the moment was should there be a national referendum to confirm the President in office? This issue and its outcome are reported on in the opening chapter of this book. But when the question was still unresolved the debate about it was at full throttle in Almaty with phrases ranging from 'This is just an old style Soviet conjuring trick' to 'We need stability that only a long term for the President can provide' ringing through the bars. By contrast the subject seemed to be barely mentioned in Astana, the company town of government.

In any city which spent most of the twentieth century under the Soviet Union, true freedom of speech and a completely free press are plants which have not yet fully taken root. But Almaty is looking promising as a garden of freedom. There are over two hundred daily newspapers and magazines published here, many of them hostile to the government although rarely critical of the President personally, a prohibition which is enshrined in the constitution. 'Even so, we have plenty of freedom of speech', says the Chairman of the 5,000 strong National Association of Journalists Seitkazy Matayev, 'what with the internet and the number of publications, we have a lot of choice, especially when you compare us to most of our neighbouring countries where there is a clampdown on the media.'

Asked why his positive view of press freedom in Kazakhstan was at odds with the negative view of Washington's Freedom House on the same issue, Mr Matayev replied, 'We get along well with Freedom House and do joint events with them. Sometimes we agree with them, for example, on the issue of libel laws which are too strict here. Sometimes we disagree with them because we think they try to apply an American template to our country using data which is not always accurate'.

Whatever the arguments may be about the limits of press freedom, there are not many criticisms of religious freedom in Almaty which is almost an over-churched and over-mosqued society. 'Objectively speaking there is a remarkable degree of religious tolerance here', says the President of Almaty's leading university, the Kazakhstan Institute of Management, Economics and Strategic Planning (KIMEP). He is Dr Chan Yong Bang, a Korean born professor who taught economics at UCLA before coming to Kazakhstan. 'Just guess how many Korean churches are flourishing in this city?' he asks. 'The answer is over fifty! There must be even more Russian orthodox churches, starting with their two cathedrals. Then you can find synagogues, Buddhist temples and most of all there are mosques, which seem to be full of young people. Although occasionally some church or pastor gets in trouble with the law, I don't think you can find serious fault with the authorities for their approval to religious inclusiveness'.

The atmosphere of freedom that prevails in Almaty has its origins in history and ethnicity. The first sizeable pretext on the national identities issue which eventually caused the break-up of the Soviet Union began in Almaty with the demonstrations of December 1986, known as *Jeltoqsan,* when students started a spontaneous march opposing the Kremlin's appointment of a Russian First Secretary. Almaty commemorates the event with an annual remembrance of those who died in the clashes. The city is not reluctant to tolerate the freedom to demonstrate on other issues today.

As for ethnicity, ever since the days of the silk road traders Almaty has been a multi-ethnic melting pot. The official statistics say that the city's population breaks down into 51 per cent Kazakhs, 30 per cent Russians, 6 per cent Uighurs, 3 per cent Koreans, 2 per cent Tatars, 1 per cent Ukranian, 1 per cent German, 1 per cent Indians, 1 per cent Chinese and 5 per cent others. But these census figures may not be entirely reliable, particularly in relation to the Chinese. Almaty is only 200 miles from the Kazakhstan's porous border with the PRC. Those who observe the city's 86 open air markets, particularly its famous Green Bazaar, believe that Chinese buyers and sellers are multiplying by the month. These trends, like the rise in mosque attendances, are interesting but they may have little long term significance other than to confirm Almaty's cosmopolitanism. But what do all these cosmopolitan inhabitants do apart from earning their living? According to Deputy Akim Serik Seidumanov, 'A remarkable number of them go to the theatre.'

*　*　*

(V) A CORNUCOPIA OF CULTURE

Almaty is a cornucopia of cultural events, facilities, composers, writers, performers, teaching academies and creative endeavours. The city claims to have 188 institutions dedicated to the arts. They include 19 theatres, 20 museums, 14 Art Galleries, 18 movie cinemas, 27 concert halls, 4 orchestras and the internationally acclaimed Abay Opera House.

'If you appreciate the arts, live in Almaty', says the famous Kazakh author and playwright Dulat Issabekov, 'this is the cradle of intelligentsia. It is a community which reveres creativity and supports it well. The average Almaty resident finds it natural to go straight from the bazaar to the performance of a play, a concert or a ballet. That's the way we live here'.

The outrages of twentieth century history showered cultural blessings on Almaty. Among the creative artists to arrive in the city were Jewish communities deported from Russia by Stalin on the pretext that they were enemies of the state. 'Now we say thank you very much Stalin for sending us so much talent', jokes Arystanbek Mukhamediuly the Rector of the Kazakh National Academy of Arts, adding that during the darkest days of the second world war complete theatre companies, orchestras and film production units were moved from Moscow to this corner of Kazakhstan in order to get them out of the way of Hitler's attacking armies.

Cultural refugees from other backgrounds also somehow gravitated to Almaty and their involvement is well represented in the city's artistic scene.

One theatre is exclusively devoted to Uighur language plays, another to German dramas, while the Korean Musical Comedy Theatre in Papanin Street is the only institution of its kind outside the borders of Korea.

Most live performances are heavily subsidized by the government, particularly in the Kazakh language theatres. So tickets for an opera or ballet at the Abay Opera House costs as little as $5 and offer an amazingly fast changing repertoire at the height of the season. In one week last June it was possible to see Swan Lake, Aida, Romeo and Juliet and The Marriage of Figaro.

Music is Almaty's crowning glory. The city's traditions of excellence in this field owe much to its Russian heritage and the teaching of Kazakh students at the Institutes of Moscow. Russian patronage was important too. Those performances at the Abay Opera House, for example, were originally well supported by the Soviet military in World War Two because its wounded officers were sent in large numbers for their convalescence to Almaty where they demanded cultural entertainment.

The Western world was surprised to discover the high quality of classical music performed in Kazakhstan after it became an independent nation. An amusing story is told about the first cultural attaché to be posted to the US embassy in Almaty in the early 1990s. Believing it was his diplomatic duty to introduce the backward nomads to the world of musical education he arranged for a visit by a group of piano teachers from the American mid-west. The teachers addressed an Almaty audience explaining a few first grade steps in scales and basic keyboard techniques. Then the Almaty musicians came to the piano and proceeded to give virtuoso performances of Beethoven's Emperor Concerto and other great works! Perhaps this tale has grown in its telling. But it is a reminder that the outside world continues to underestimate the talent that is trained by the city's principal academies and institutes.

Jania Aubakirova is Rector of the Kazakh National Conservatory which is named after the composer Kurmangazy Sagyrbayuly. In her early career she was an internationally acclaimed concert pianist but she has concentrated for the past fifteen years in developing the highest standards for the students at the institution she leads. They are, by forms of measurement, better taught, better funded and more numerous than in many of their European equivalents. As she explains:

'Our Conservatory now has 700 students. They each get an annual scholarship grant of 1 million KZT ($US 6,850) and we receive an annual budget from the government of 848 million KZT (US$5.8 million), which has risen sharply from 60 million KZT (US$400,000) since I became Rector in 1997. We teach all musical disciplines and instruments. Our teacher pupil ratio is one to three which astonishes most European musical academies because they usually have about one teacher to every ten pupils'.

Jania Aubakirova says in recent years her conservatory has educated some fifteen world class musicians who regularly perform as soloists in the concert halls of major international capitals. More importantly, the Kazakh National Conservatory provides most of the professional musicians for the country's four major orchestras who are also gaining international recognition by their performances in venues such as Washington's Kennedy Centre, London's Barbican and the Paris Opera. These successes are mainly in the field of traditional classical music but there is growing global appreciation for modern Kazakh music.

'We are the pioneers in opening up Kazakhstan's music to the world', says Jania Aubakirova, 'we used to look only towards Europe and America. But now we look more and more towards Asia, Japanese and Korean audiences who love Kazakh music which is spacious and untamed in its originality, with considerable improvisation.'

Any music lover attending a Kazakh concert for the first time will find it easy to be captivated by the unusual sounds and rhythms of the country's traditional instruments such as the dombra, kobyz, saz syrnai and zhetigen. Modern works by Kazakh composers are often evocative of the steppes and the nomadic culture of wild horses, eagles, mountains and vast open spaces.

The first time I began to appreciate the richness of the country's contemporary music was when I attended a Kazakh gala concert at London's Guildhall in 2008. It was an evening when the Royal Philharmonic Orchestra was conducted by a brilliant 27 year old,

Marius Stravinsky, whose exotic Kazakh roots and musical history are as fascinating as his formidable talent.

Marius Stravinsky was born in Almaty in 1979 – a year of frightening food shortages in the Soviet Union. His father was a Lithuanian concert pianist who like many Soviet artists had been exiled to the city then called Alma-Ata. There he wooed and won the young woman who was thought of as one of Kazakhstan's greatest beauties and most gifted pianists. She was Eleonora Bekova from a village near Karaganda, one of three child prodigy Bekova sisters. After their training at the Moscow Conservatoire, the three became internationally known for their performances across the Soviet Union and Western Europe.

Eleonora's fame as a musician guaranteed her son a place at the Moscow Central Music School. Marius entered it at the age of four, showing outstanding promise as a violinist. But the Bekova family's status suddenly fell into political disgrace with the Soviet authorities when one of the sisters, Alfia, defected to the West while on a concert tour of Britain. Eventually, Eleonora was given permission in the more relaxed Gorbachev era of *Perestroika*, to join her sister in exile.

Accompanying his mother, Marius Stravinsky resumed his violin studies at the Yehudi Menuhin School in London, later winning a music scholarship to Eton. During his five years as an Etonian he was encouraged by the Precentor, Ralph Allwood, to conduct the school orchestra. This started a new passion for conducting which led to Stravinsky attending the Royal Academy of Music in Britain. Later he returned to the Moscow Conservatoire as a conductor and formed his own orchestra of fellow students.

Recognition for Stravinsky's skills with the baton came with his appointment as chief conductor of Russia's Karelia Orchestra, followed by a steady flow of guest conductor appearances in his native Kazakhstan. 'I love the diaconic harmonies of Kazakh music as it evokes the rhythms and sounds of the steppes and the nomad heritage' says Stravinsky. He is one of an elite group of internationally acclaimed Kazakh performers who originate from or were trained in Almaty. The city is a particular nursery of musical talent, but this is part of a deeper and wider cultural energy.

From its concerts to its art galleries, public buildings, sculptures and gardens, Almaty is a centre of creativity and beauty. It was for many years the most extrovert and exciting crossroads of Central Asia as well as being the *de facto* capital of independent Kazakhstan.

But suddenly, in 1994, Almaty's confidence was hit by an unusual shock from an unexpected quarter. The blow fell on 6 July 1994 when President Nazarbayev announced to an astonished Parliament and public that a new national capital was to be built eight hundred miles away in Astana.

* * *

(VI) ENTER ASTANA

Astana was born as the new national capital before Almaty knew of its rejection. Paradoxically the President who made the controversial decision was emotionally and personally attached to the losing city. He loved its beauty, its cosmopolitan culture, its imposing public buildings and its jewel like setting on the edge of the Alatau mountains. But those mountains were a barrier to the expansion of Almaty. Nazarbayev was dreaming of a capital city proclaiming the symbolism of a newly independent nation. He wanted to build a parliament, a supreme court, a ministry of defence, a ministry of foreign affairs, a diplomatic quarter and a presidential palace. But there was no room for such expansionism in Almaty which, thanks to its encirclement by mountains, was already the most congested and polluted conurbation of Central Asia with an airport that was fog or smog bound for over 60 days a year.

In addition to these environmental and ecological objectives to Almaty there were other unspoken problems. It was in style and substance a city with a Soviet atmosphere. Some Kazakhs felt uncomfortable there. There was also a strategic anxiety about creating a capital in the south east corner of the country just two hundred miles from the border with China. Taking all these factors into account Nazarbayev put aside his personal preference for Almaty and favoured a relocation of the centre of government to some other part of Kazakhstan. But where?

After a thorough examination of all the options, a sleepy northern town, Akmola, was chosen to be the new national capital. Its name translated, some thought appropriately, as 'The White Tombstone'. Although in the 1950s it had briefly enjoyed some Soviet architectural development because Nikita Krushev designated it as the centre of an ill fated agricultural project known as the Virgin Lands Scheme. Akmola had been a moribund if not a dying city after the project failed. But its symbolic location at the heart of the steppes, its good rail links to cities all over Central Asia and its scope for unlimited development had an almost mystical appeal to Nazarbayev. Where pessimists saw a cold decrepit and isolated one horse town, the optimistic President saw a shining new national capital rising on the banks of the pictur-esque Ishym river with futuristic architecture that would make it the Manhattan of Eurasia.

No-one else shared this vision least of all in Almaty where the project was openly ridiculed. Opinion polls showed that sixty-two per cent of the city's population opposed the plan to transfer the government to the far north of the country. Many of those in the 'No' camp were state employees who feared that their quality of life would be downgraded when they uprooted from sophisticated Almaty to primitive Akmola. Initially they were right. For the first four or five years of its existence the emerging national capital was a nightmarish building site. Its construction was fraught with problems. The area was hot and windy in summer while the winters were as arctic as Siberia's, made worse by notorious snowstorms known as *buran*. Power failures, cash flow shortages and design faults compounded the difficulties which were only overcome by massive injections of government money and Presidential will power.

Many strategic decisions had to be taken and implemented in the mid 1990s if Akmola was going to be changed from a sleepy provincial backwater into an international capital. One symbolic move was a name change. Akmola not only had an unfelicitous linguistic meaning of

'The White Tomb' or alternatively 'The Deadly Winter'. The town and its surrounding area was also associated with prison camps, mosquito plagues, high winds and the economic failure of the Virgin Lands Scheme. Nazarbayev was sensitive towards the need to make a clean break with the past. There were suggestions that the city should be called Sary Arka (the heart of the steppes), Ishym (after the river) or even Nursultan. Nazarbayev himself came up with Astana. The word in Kazakh is a subtle one, implying the flight of an eagle, or a winged journey into the future. However, Nazarbayev selected it for unsubtle reason. For the name literally means 'capital'. There were wags in Almaty who said that in the same spirit of originality it might as well be called 'railway junction' or 'city'. But Nazarbayev stanchly defended his choice as 'the perfect name for the capital – distinct, easy to pronounce, understandable in all languages'.

Within weeks of his pronouncement Akmola was renamed Astana by presidential decree. On 10 June 1998 the new national capital was officially inaugurated with a presentation day of elaborate ceremonies and speeches. The President's dream had come true. Astana was open for business.

* * *

(VII) THE CREATION OF AN INTERNATIONAL CAPITAL

Nearly two decades have passed since President Nazarbayev made his startling announcement to the parliament then sitting in Almaty that he was planning to create a new capital of Kazakhstan. Most of his audience were at best sceptical and at worst angry about the proposal. But now the critics are confounded. Whether they liked the original idea or loathed it, whether they have resented or admired the city's grandiose building plans, the reality today is that Astana is not only here to stay, it has become independent Kazakhstan's greatest success story.

Astana, now a thriving city of over 750,000, is one of the world's most unusual and idiosyncratic capitals. It is packed with surprises.

If a group of strangers were blindfolded, flown to it and asked on opening their eyes, 'Where do you think you are?' their answers might begin with 'fairyland' or 'the set of a movie' and then move through a guessing game of countries and continents. For the exotic skyline is dominated by buildings so disparate in their shapes and sizes, contours and colours, traditions and trajectories that consistency is to be found nowhere, while unorthodoxy rules everywhere. Even more startling than the diversity of design is the discovery that there was one dominant decision-maker who instructed the planners and architects, selected the colour schemes, sketched his own drawings for many of the important buildings and conceptualized the entire city. This decision-maker was Nazarbayev.

A good place to enter the mindset of Nazarbayev in his role as creator-in-chief of Astana is Baiterek, a ninety-seven metre tower sprouting from the heart of the central boulevard. Originally sketched out in the President's own hand, it is a modernistic representation of the tree of life, *Baiterek*, at whose apex stands a glass sphere and a gold ball portraying the Kazakh national myth of a golden egg laid by the legendary bird, *Samruk*. The viewing platform is bisected by the Ishym River into left-bank and right-bank sectors. The right bank is the so-called old city, although precious little in the way of antiquity has been left standing apart from a handful of institutional edifices from the Tsarist and Communist eras. The left bank is where Nazarbayev's vision for the new capital takes wing, since almost every building has been erected since the new capital was inaugurated in 1998

One of the more conservative of the temporary creations in Astana is the presidential palace, Akorda, an approximate yet highly imaginative reproduction of America's White House. Much larger in size than its original inspiration in Washington DC, it is topped by a bright blue dome and a needle-like spire. If President Nazarbayev looks out of his office window in Akorda he sees two landmark buildings on the skyline which were created by the British architect Norman Foster.

The first is Khan Shatyr, the world's largest tent. From the outside it is a 150 metre high re-creation of a nomad leader's camp complete with wigwam-style struts pointing towards the sky and rolling billows of transparent tenting material cascading to ground level like a see through dancers dress swirling down from neck to ankles.

This material absorbs all climatic changes from heavy snow to sweltering sunlight. So inside Khan Shatyr there is a mild summer temperature all year round even when the exterior weather is ranging from +40 to −30 degrees Celsius.

The size of this 'King's Tent' is an area larger than a football stadium's. Its nine floors reproduce cobbled streets and squares; sandy beaches; swimming pools; golf courses; leisure parks and shopping malls.

Expensive but enjoyable, Khan Shatyr perpetrates the illusion that Astanaland is fantasyland. The same can be said of the other and earlier, Norman Foster creation in the capital. This is a one hundred metre high steel and glass pyramid which doubles up as a conference centre, concert hall venue for international summits and a major tourist attraction. The pyramids official title is 'The Palace of Peace and Reconciliation'. This last word would be inappropriate to apply to the architecture on the left bank since both the styles and the substance of the most prominent skyscrapers are irreconcilable. They include: A matching pair of circular towers known to locals as 'the golden ice-cream cones'; a national archives building in the shape of a grey-green egg; a mustard-coloured international business centre; a gargantuan 5,000-residence Soviet-style colossus in the clouds which is an exact replica of Moscow's State University; a bronze glass multi-storey building with a hinge on top which locals call 'the cigarette lighter'; a UFO-style spaceship which plays host to circuses and festivals; a boat-shaped 3,000-seat concert hall; an Arabian mosque; massive ministerial offices with gold window panes; the upper and lower houses of Parliament and as far as the eye can see, more and more high-rise buildings in every imaginable tradition and fashion, from the banal to the bizarre.

The mind and the eye soon start reeling on a tour of Astana. The layout of the city is conventional, but the mixture of colours and building styles resembles a mosaic of eccentricity. Jumbled up together without planning rhyme or reason are Manhattan apartment blocks,

Muscovite onion domes, Dutch windmills, French chateaux, Byzantine cupolas, Middle Eastern minarets, Chinese pagodas, Turkish bazaars, Tuscan villas, Japanese restaurants, Corinthian columns, Scandinavian convention hotels, Hong Kong high rises, Russian orthodox churches, Spanish haciendas, Korean supermarkets, Mexican wave glass skyscrapers, Stalinist office blocks in the monolithic manner of 1930s Moscow and American shopping malls which could have been plucked straight from twenty-first century California.

Although there are jarring juxtapositions aplenty in this extraordinary metropolis, the cumulative effect of all these contrasts and experiments is that Astana feels alive. It is a young, energetic city whose inhabitants have an average age of thirty-two. If, in summer, a traveller strolls through the parks or visits the massive statues dedicated to such themes as 'victims of totalitarianism' or 'warriors of the Junghar invasions', the multiplicity of languages spoke around them brings to mind the Tower of Babel. The same phenomenon prevails in shops and supermarkets, where the variety of the international produce is as exotic as the variety of local architecture. But Astana is a confluence not a clash of cultures. For the peoples that have flocked to come and live in the new capital are drawn from a kaleidoscope of nationalities. Only sixty per cent of Kazakhstanis are Kazakhs. The remainder come from one hundred identifiable ethnic groups of which the most prominent are Russians, Ukrainians, Uzbeks, Koreans, Germans, Uighurs, Chechens, Poles, Crimeans, Tartars, Turks, Greeks, Persians, Kyrgyz, Turkmen and Chinese. The novelty of Astana has helped them all to feel at home.

*　*　*

(VIII) THE FUTURE OF ASTANA

But where is this home and what is its future? Astana is set in the continents of Europe and Asia. It is near nowhere. If you fly south-east, eventually you reach Almaty after 1,200 kilometres. If you fly west, the first city of any size is Atyrau, centre of the Caspian oil industry, some 1,600 kilometres away. Travelling due north, there is a vast expanse of emptiness punctuated only by endless wheat fields, occasional farming villages and two small provincial towns. To the north-east lies Siberia. A north-west course takes you to Moscow, a three and a half hour flight away. In between these points of the compass lies Sary Arka, the Great Steppe, a colossal wilderness of both flat and mountainous grassland traditionally regarded as the ancestral region of the Kazakh nomads. Creating a national capital in such a remote and inhospitable area was widely regarded as mission impossible when the project started. Now that it has become mission successful – even though much more will be accomplished – the forthcoming twentieth anniversary of the country offers a good moment for reflection on what Astana means to Kazakhstan today and to future generations.

Astana was created for a mixture of motives. Did it represent a visionary seat of government for a twenty-first century nation? The essential re-location of an overcrowded former national capital whose infrastructure was inadequate? A new strategic crossroads for Eurasia? A presidential folly of extravagant hubris? A financially over-extended conglomeration of uncompleted apartment blocks? A political safety bunker designed to put Kazakhstan's power structures as far away as possible from the borders of potential invaders? A regional hub of futuristic industries and transport links? A return to the emotional roots of Kazakhstan's history and culture in the heartlands of the steppes? Some, none or all of the above?

As a seat of government Astana has bedded down more swiftly than its nineteenth and twentieth century equivalents across the world such as Washington DC, Ottawa, Canberra, Brasilia or Bonn. All of these artificially created seats of government took longer to gain national and international acceptance, while one of them (Bonn) has lost its capital city status. This is a reminder that although a government can build a new capital it cannot always make it work quickly or permanently. Yet Astana undoubtedly is working for at least three good reasons that are peculiar to Kazakhstan.

First, the nation believes it is more strategically secure because of the existence of Astana. Today it looks fanciful to fear an invasion by foreign armies. But in the more volatile political atmosphere of the early 1990s when Kazakhstan had no agreed borders with either Russia or China, a land grab by either potential aggressor was not such an absurd nightmare. In particular there were Moscow campaigners including Aleksandr Solzhenitsyn in his notorious pamphlet on the subject, who argued that the empty northern lands of Kazakhstan should rightly belong to Russia. Thanks to the creation of Astana those northern lands are now populated by a major city. Its existence, backed up by the combination of agreed borders and good relations with Russia and China (*see chapter 8*), means that Kazakhstan need have no fears about predatory troubles from its mighty neighbours.

Secondly, Astana has redressed the country's population imbalance, which was once too heavily weighted towards Almaty and the southeast region. This rebalancing act is not just a matter of numbers. In the complex tribal make up of the Kazakhs consisting of Great, Small and Middle *zhuzs*, the creation of Astana has softened some historic traditions and attracted many thousands of Khazakhstanis from multiethnic backgrounds to the new capital.

Thirdly, Astana has carved out its own niche as a spectacular venue for international conferences and sporting events. In the last few months alone the city has hosted the OSCE Summit (*see chapter 9*) and the opening ceremonies of the 2011 Asian Winter Games. The first was a triumph of both diplomacy and logistics as 56 world leaders including Hillary Clinton, Angela Merkel, Nicolas Sarkozy, Silvia Berlusconi and Dmitri Medvedev descended on the capital. Whatever the international results of this two day conference, the domestic impact was immensely positive. Ordinary Kazakhstanis were overflowing with patriotic pride as they watched the comings, goings and speechmaking of the international VIPs. For the days of the conference, 1–2 December 2010, ordinary life almost stopped in the country as most people stayed glued to their television sets. It was a moment when Kazakhstan felt it had come of age as a serious player on the world stage.

Under the leadership of its dynamic Akim Imangali Tasmagambetov, Astana does conferences well and has now had plenty of practice in organizing them. Some of its venues are spectacular, notably the Great Pyramid *aka* the Palace of Peace and Reconciliation which is a permanent venue for the triennial congress of World and Traditional Religions and for regional events such as meetings of the Shanghai Cooperation Council. The grandest addition to the capital's showpieces is the 30,000 seat Astana Arena, completed just in time for the launch of the 2011 Asian Winter Games. The opening ceremony of this competition was an extraordinary extravaganza of torchlight processions, high-tech stagecraft, laser pyrotechnics and firework displays on an epic scale. Somewhere in Astana there must be a tribe of would-be Hollywood directors striving to re-create on the steppes a galaxy of special effects to rival *Star Wars* or *Avatar*.

Mega productions on this scale cost many millions of dollars. Yet they are a surprisingly frequent feature of the Astana calendar. This revolves around a number of anniversary or special events ranging from the President's Birthday on 6 July (also Astana Day) to international sports tournaments and political conferences. Many of these festivities have a flavour of the Roman Empire's legendary games, chariot races and circuses. The similar enthusiasm of Kazakhstan's crowds for ornate opening ceremonies, colourful sports competitions and folkloric festivals seems to be making the statement: 'We are a new nation. We are proud of our nomadic culture. We have always been hospitable. Now we are rich. So we are showing off in order to prove that anything our neighbours can do, we can do better'.

Astana's latest architecture has set the tone for a further era of ostentatious flamboyance. Among the newest or coming innovations are a National Academy of Music built in the shape of a grand piano and a 33,000 square metre National Library which combines a circular arch, rotunda and yurt in the form of a gigantic Moebius strip. A visitor surveying the city's skyline will have a number of reactions to the shapes, sizes and styles, of the amazing editions in this wonderland of varieties which range across a huge spectrum of taste from Disneyworld Kitsch to Wagnerian Valhalla. But surprise is likely to be a constant factor. Every time I visit Astana, I remember the astonished comment of the Queen of Sheba when she arrived at the court of King Solomon 'Behold, the half was not told me'.

Of course, not every Kazakhstani agrees with this epic development in Astana over the pasttwelve years. One of the leaders of the opposition party Azat, Bulat Abilov, may well echo the thoughts of some residents of other regions when he says, 'The fact is that one city is being developed at the expense of everywhere else'.

Another point of view is that the showpiece architecture of Astana has acted as a spur to other conurbations. Several of them are leaping in their civic development from a Soviet to a futuristic approach. This is becoming increasingly true of Almaty which has been inspired to create a glittering centre of skyscrapers and the region's first subway system.

The competitive spirit between Kazakhstan's first and second cities has some way to go. Yet in the long run Astana is likely to become the clear winner. Its easy availability of development land and its primacy as the seat of national government are advantages which will prove unbeatable. The greatest advantage of all is the determined enthusiasm of its founding father to put economic power and creative originality into the new city. As a result the variegated mosaic and momentum of Astana produces many more cheers than criticisms. It is one of the wonders of the twenty-first century which puts Kazakhstan on the map and Central Asia on the agenda, of the modern world. It took extraordinary political will power and creative vision to invent such a national capital. The credit for it must go to the Kazakhstani President. As his fellow President Dimitri Medvedev of Russia said in an eloquent tribute at the tenth anniversary celebrations, 'Nursultan Nazarbayev has given this city not only his work but also his soul ... truly it may be said "Astana is his child"'.

7

After the Recession –
Prospects for the Economy

(I) HOW THE RECOVERY SUCCEEDED

Kazakhstan was hit hard and early by the global recession of 2008-9. Its over extended banks were paralysed, surviving only by government bailout. Its over ambitious construction industry went into free fall, symbolized by the Astana and Almaty skylines of unfinished apartment blocks and mothballed cranes. Unemployment soared and confidence plummeted. It was not quite a return to the bread queues and soup kitchens of the post independence traumas but GDP growth slumped to 1.2 per cent and falling in mid 2009. With oil prices falling too, economic meltdown looked uncomfortably close.

But just when the pessimists were predicting the worst of times, Kazakhstan turned the corner towards the best of times. It recovered faster than any western economy and most Asian ones. By the middle of 2011 the indicators showed a return to annualized GDP growth of seven per cent, unemployment falling below five per cent, a trade surplus running at over $30 billion and cash reserves of $68 billion. How was this turnaround achieved? The answer seems to be a combination of good luck, good management and good people.

'Yes we did have the good luck of oil prices and other national resource prices climbing back to high levels in a short time', says Grigory Marchenko, the Central Bank Governor who played a key role in the recovery strategy, 'but we also recognized the problem early; we dipped into the National Fund quite boldly; we took the right corrective measures such as devaluation and expenditure reductions; we were fortunate that the crisis turned out to be a relatively short one'.

This thumbnail sketch is accurate but it does not do justice to the political will power that was needed to see the strategy through. Those responsible for the policy came under heavy fire from critical public opinion. 'I had to ask my elderly parents to stop reading newspapers for some months!'recalled Marchenko. Prime Minister Karim Massimov faced calls for his resignation. Even the Teflon President Nazarbayev who usually manages to rise above the fray of political controversy by being constitutionally protected from personal attack as Head of State, nevertheless came in for sharp criticism as banks tottered and budgets were cut. But the medicine worked.

The pain of the cure was softened by heavy government borrowing and cash subsidies from the national sovereign wealth fund. 'We spent $19 billion dollars to overcome the crisis, with $10 billion of it coming from the National Fund. A key ingredient in our strategy was the availability of money', said Marchenko.

The National Fund had been created in 2000 as a result of Nazarbayev's examination of various models in other countries, particularly Norway. The strongest view among the President's advisors in those days had been that Kazakhstan should *not* create the fund. They thought the oil revenues should be used immediately in the cause of developing the country. But Nazarbayev was impressed by the more cautious approach of the Norwegians who set aside part of their oil revenues in case of the proverbial rainy day. It was just as well that the President's view prevailed, for when the recessionary rain came down heavily in 2008–9, Kazakhstan's National Fund provided the vital lifeline of hard cash.

To say that Kazakhstan spent its way out of recession would be wrong because stringent reductions were made in departmental budgets and the Tenge was devalued by twenty-five per cent. But at the same time expenditure was increased on infrastructure projects which aimed to create 350,000 new jobs in areas such as agricultural irrigation schemes, sewage works, water reservoirs, meat processing plants, schools, hospitals and a 3,000 mile Western Europe to Western China motor-rail transit corridor.

These measures worked because of politics as much as economics. President Nazarbayev, who had steered the country through two previous crises in 1991–2 and 1998–9, gave a strong lead to his ministers and to the country. In a national television broadcast delivered on 6 March 2009, he unveiled the list of infrastructure projects to the public; reminded them that Kazakhstan's gold and currency reserves plus the assets of the National Fund stood at a combined total of over

$51 billion; and ended with an emotional appeal to repeat earlier achievements of nation-building.

'It was during our most difficult years when we began and completed construction of a new national capital – Astana – at a time when no-one believed we would be able to do that. Let us now emulate that positive experience'.

The Astana spirit has passed in to the national legends of Kazakhstan rather as the Dunkirk spirit has become part of Britain's folklore. Nazarbayev played a strong card when he evoked it in his speech. A few weeks earlier he had told Prime Minister Massimov and other senior ministers.

'It's time you banged your fist on the table and started working abnormally ... I am giving you carte blanche to stabilise the economy and the financial system as well as wide powers to make unorthodox decisions ... I instruct you that it is better to make a decision than to be afraid to make a mistake'.

The economic triumvirate of ministers in charge of managing the economy took this Presidential instruction to heart. They were Prime Minister Karim Massimov, a high performing former Transport Minister of Uigur ethnic background; Finance Minister Bolat Zhamishev a workaholic technocrat described by Almaty economists as 'the safest of safe pair of hands', and the intellectually impressive Central Bank Governor Grigory Marchenko. Nazarbayev kept faith with them throughout the worst of the turbulence. They were re-appointed to their posts at the start of his new term of office in April 2011. That continuity says much for their competence which in turn has resulted in growing national and international confidence in Kazakhstan's recovery. But for all the good management and good personnel, the economy would not have bounced back so quickly without the huge bonus of rising oil prices and increasing oil production.

* * *

(II) OIL POWER – YESTERDAY, TODAY AND TOMORROW

When President Nazarbayev and Prime Minister Massimov were hammering out the country's economic strategy in the depths of recession they based their calculations on the premise that oil prices would fall to $40 a barrel. At the time of writing (August 2011) world oil prices are over $100 a barrel. What is also rising is Kazakhstan's position in the world league table of oil producing countries. Today with production of 1.6 million barrels per day Kazakhstan is in the No 48 position in the league, but in the coming decade it will leap forward to the top ten and probably to the top five.

According to many expert sources, most notably the authoritative report of the United States Energy Information Agency published in November 2010, Kazakhstan will more than double its oil production by 2019 and become the fifth largest oil producing country in the world. 'Full development of its major oil fields could make Kazakhstan one of the world's five oil producers within the decade', says the EIA, noting that the continued development of its giant Tengiz, Karachaganak and Kashagan fields would put Kazakhstan in the top tier of Saudi Arabia, Russia, the United States and Kuwait.

Although there are some question marks and technical difficulties hanging over the speed at which Kazakhstan will develop its giant new fields in the Caspian, the EIA and other similar predictions confirm that Kazakhstan is fast becoming a giant player in the new 'great game' of global oil power. How did this happen? What does it mean for the country and for its future?

Kazakhstanis like to say that they have been producing oil for over a hundred years. This was historically true but commercially insignificant for the first eighty years of that century. Until Kazakhstan became independent in 1991 its oil production under the control of the Soviet Oil Ministry was miniscule.

One of the few people who knew the secret that Kazakhstan's territory contained huge oil reserves was Nazarbayev – and he found out by accident. In June 1985, a year after he had been appointed Prime

Minister of the Soviet Republic of Kazakhstan, he was told that there had been a blow out at a remote onshore borehole, known as T-37, in the Guriev district of the Caspian region. When drilling was in progress on this site, oil was not only struck, it exploded into a gusher which sent a gigantic fountain of raw crude shooting 150 metres above the surface and bursting into flames. For the next thirteen months the greatest experts and the most experienced fire fighting units from all over the Soviet Union struggled unsuccessfully to bring this disaster under control. Eventually the Texan expert Red Adair capped the blazing well four hundred days after the original explosion with an estimated thirty-four million barrels of oil burnt off in the inferno.

Although as a novice Prime Minister of a Soviet satellite Republic Nazarbayev was never well briefed on the high pressure reserves that had caused the catastrophe – the worst in the history of the Soviet oil industry – the episode left its mark on him in several important ways. It was the first clue that the oil field, known as Tengiz, on the Caspian shores of Kazakhstan could have enormous potential. He also saw clearly that the oil ministry of the Soviet Union was far too backward in its technical and managerial expertise to exploit a field of this magnitude. 'I realised there was no modern technology of the USSR to develop a huge field such as Tengiz', said Nazarbayev. 'I knew that one day we would have to turn to Western oil companies to reverse the neglect of our energy reserves'.

In the last year of the Soviet Union's existence, development discussions about Tengiz between the oil ministry in Moscow and the American oil company Chevron became deadlocked. Nazarbayev seized his moment. He persuaded Gorbachev to transfer the authority for the Tengiz negotiations away from the Soviet Oil Minister to the Republic of Kazakhstan's Council of Ministers. This persuasion was not a delicate operation. 'Kazakhstan will henceforth take control of the field', wrote Nazarbayev in an imperious letter to Gorbachev in July 1991. Ostensibly the Soviet leader went along with this blatant grab for power on the grounds that Kazakhstan's negotiators would be able to extract better terms from Chevron. A more probable explanation was that Nazarbayev,

'You are one of the model leaders of the world. We could not have this summit without your presence.' President Obama welcoming President Nazarbayev to Washington DC for the 2010 Nuclear Security Summit

Kazakhstan, the first Asian and Islamic nation to hold the Presidency of the OSCE, hosts 56 world leaders at the organisation's 2010 summit in Astana

Almaty born Marius Stravinsky (27) conducting the Royal Philharmonic Orchestra at the 2007 Kazakh Gala Concert in London

President Nazarbayev is interviewed by author Jonathan Aitken

Visiting Stepnogorsk Prison
Jonathan Aitken with group of Correctional Officers

President Nazarbayev inaugurates a new petrochemical plant at the Tengiz Oil field. Kazakhstan now produces 1.7 million barrels of oil per day and is expected to become one of the five biggest oil producing nations in the world by 2015

Agriculture is becoming a major force in Kazakhstan's economy and exports as the country's 155,000 farms switch to US methods and machinery

Old Almaty: The Government Administration Building which in Soviet times was the headquarters of the Communist Party

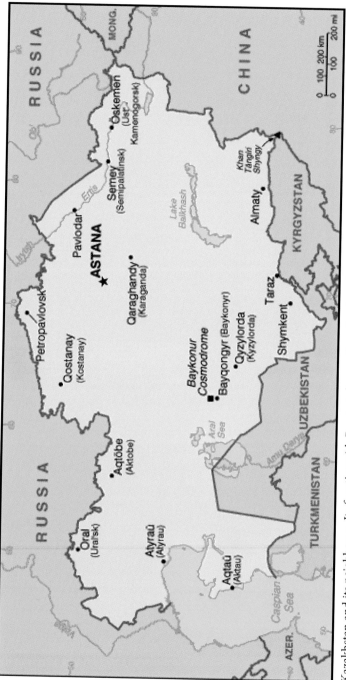

Kazakhstan and its neighbours. Its frontier with Russia is longer than the Canada-US land border

as a senior Politburo member, was using the leverage of his position by bidding to control the Caspian negotiations at a time of extreme vulnerability for the leadership of the Soviet Union. Gorbachev badly needed Nazarbayev's help with the divided leaders of the Republic's about a new Union treaty. The help was given. But the covert *quid pro quo* was that Kazakhstan should take over the deal making with Chevron.

Nazarbayev, who is a workaholic master of detail, proved adept at negotiating with Chevron, even using the agreement to extract political terms from President George H. W. Bush on wider issues. The eventual foundation document that was signed in 1992 has proved to be a great deal for both sides. Known as Tengizchevroil or TCO the company, whose profits are split 80–20 in Kazakhstan's favour, has in the last fifteen years produced over 120 million tonnes of oil, five billion cubic metres of gas and revenues to Kazakhstan of over $20 billion. The field now produces over 500,000 barrels of oil a day, which the Energy Information Agency report of 2010 forecasts will rise to 800,000 barrels of oil a day within five years.

Tengiz, an onshore field, is not the greatest of the jewels in Kazakhstan's oil crown. These lie offshore beneath the waters of the Caspian Sea. But they remained untouchable until the early years of the twenty-first century. This was because Russia was so impossibly intransigent over the offshore rights negotiations, pretending for several years that the Caspian was an inland lake rather than a sea. Almost every month between 1992 and 1998 there was a meeting of the five Caspian littoral countries attended by Foreign Ministers or their Deputies. As Erlan Idrissov, who was Kazakhstan's representative at these marathons of tedium has recalled:

'Progress at these meetings was negligible. We wasted years going round in circles with no hope of an agreement and no chance of a drop of oil coming out of the Caspian while this deadlock lasted. It was only when President Nazarbayev stepped in and negotiated face to face with President Yeltsin that we found a solution'.

The deadlock was broken during what is now called 'the night of napkin diplomacy'. This was a private dinner in Zavidovo, Yeltsin's hunting lodge one hundred miles east of Moscow on the night of 5 July

1998. Good personal chemistry and good vodka made their contribution to the cordiality of the evening. Having persuaded his host that an offshore oil rights agreement would benefit Russia as much as Kazakhstan, Nazarbayev started a detailed discussion of the sea bed share-out.

He took hold of a table napkin and began drawing on it a sketch map of the northern Caspian. This napkin has been preserved for posterity in a museum in Astana. Historians may have difficulty in deciphering the post prandial hieroglyphics of the two leaders, but at the time their intentions were clear and an agreement was reached.

The nocturnal accord was converted by daylight into the text of an official announcement. The aides who did this vital work were Yeltsin's principal assistant Sergei Prihod'ko and Nazarbayev's chief of staff, Nurtai Abikayev.

'From 2 a.m. until 9 a.m., Prihod'ko and I used our notes and the drawings on the napkin to draft the text of a joint statement by the two Presidents', recalled Abikayev. 'This was the declaration of intent to delineate the seabed borders of the Caspian in accordance with a median line modified by the two Presidents'.

The importance of the 'napkin agreement' was that it cleared the way for exploration of the Caspian's oil prospects to begin. This soon unlocked riches which were to prove far greater than Nazarbayev had dreamed of at the time.

The first manifestation of this bonanza came when oil was struck in May 2000 at Kashagan, a new offshore field forty-eight miles south east of Atyrau. It has turned out to be the world's largest discovery for forty years, second in size only to Saudi Arabia's legendary Ghawar oil field. Kashagan is now estimated by the EIA to contain at least fourteen billion barrels of recoverable reserves. This makes it an even larger field than the onshore Tengiz which has reserves of nine billion barrels. Adding in the country's six other largest oil fields, the EIA's calculation is that Kazakhstan has at least thirty billion barrels of proven reserves.

The speed at which the mammoth Kashagan field will come on stream is a matter of intense speculation within the international oil industry. The consortium led by ENI of Italy has encountered severe technical problems and there are also disputes of considerable legal complexity in the turbulent waters of the Caspian between the consortium partners and the government. Although these tensions are likely to delay the start date of Kashagan production to 2013 for phase one and until 2020 for phase two there is no doubt that its offshore oil, when added to the existing onshore oil production, will move Kazakhstan into the top ten and then the top five of the world's largest oil powers.

To understand how this massive flow of oil wealth is being managed I visited a landmark building in Astana universally known as 'The Silo'. It is the headquarters of the national oil and gas company KazMunaiGas and also contains the office of the Oil Minister Sauat Mynbaev. As an architectural showpiece it resembles a modernistic Arc de Triomphe with two outstretched wings of gold and copper coloured windows. Driving up to it you feel as though you are approaching an imperial gateway created in honour of the power of money.

The aura of power continues inside the building but the structures of responsibility are somewhat complex. KazMunaiGas is a huge oil and gas company in its own right, producing around 400,000 barrels of oil per day, owning twenty per cent of the Chevron led Tengiz chevroil consortium and operating the new Kashagan field with its western partners headed by ENI.

The day to day management decisions of KazMunaiGas are taken by its Director General Kairgeldy Kabyldin. He talks interestingly about production statistics, the development of existing fields and the expansion of KazMunaiGas into the EU through its purchase of a Romanian company which owned refineries and fifteen hundred filling stations in seven European countries. However Kabyldin is reluctant to answer questions on policy or strategy issues, pointing out that one hundred per cent of KazMunaiGas shares are owned by the national holding company Samruk-Kazyna.

President Nazarbayev's son-in-law, Timur Kulibayev is both Chairman of KazMunaiGas and Chairman of Samruk-Kazyna. An able and energetic businessman Kulibayev has a track record of success in the private sector which has earned him (according to Forbes Magazine) a personal net worth of over $2 billion. Today he is probably the most powerful figure after the President in directing the future of Kazakhstan's oil and gas industries. As the final section of this chapter shows, Kulibayev is now playing a key strategic role in the country's economic future as chairman of the country's sovereign wealth fund which, in addition to the oil and gas industries, controls over four hundred state owned companies.

Another key voice in this power structure is that of the Oil Minister Sauat Mynbaev. His office also occupies part of the golden silo. He is a good example of the rising meritocracy and technocracy at the heart of the government of Kazakhstan.

Born in 1962 as the sixth child of a village schoolteacher in Eastern Kazakhstan, Mynbaev won his way by scholarships to Moscow State University where he graduated in Economic Cybernetics, a subject he taught as an academic professor at the Almaty Institute of National Economy in the late 1980s. As free markets began to dawn at the time of independence, Mynbaev gave up his modest teaching salary to enter the world of business. Starting as a market-maker between commodity buyers and sellers, he became President of the Almaty Stock Exchange and owner of KazKommerz Bank. In this position he made a large private fortune. He also developed a public profile by writing critical articles in newspapers about the government's lack of policy in its management of foreign debt.

Soon afterwards in 1995 Mynbaev was invited to join the government. He served in various positions including Deputy Minister of Finance, Deputy Head of the Presidential Administration, Minister of Agriculture and Deputy Prime Minister. As Minister for Oil and Gas he supervises not only the country's oil production but also its fast expanding network of pipelines which will transform the transporting and selling of the country's oil. 'Much more of our oil exports will go to Europe after 2013', says Mynbaev 'today we produce approximately eighty million tonnes of which some thirteen million is used by the domestic market, seven million goes to China and the rest is exported on north bound pipelines via Russia. But all is changing as a result of our new pipelines to China, across the Black Sea to Europe and our tankers across the Caspian to Baku and Tbilisi'.

From such optimistic interviews and from visiting the booming Caspian oil cities of Aktau and Atyrau, it is easy to see that Kazakhstan is creating one of the twenty-first century's most important strategic hubs for the production and transportation of oil and gas. It will rival the Arabian and Persian Gulf in its significance to world supplies. The estimated future spend on the country's three main fields of Tengiz, Karachaganak and Kashagan is foreign investment of over $120 billion and expected annual production from these areas of 150 million tonnes of oil. The prospects for Kazakhstan look amazing but can anything go wrong?

One clue that there are problems in the way of these golden dreams is the industry insiders' nickname for the country's largest field. They call it 'Cash all gone'. This is a reference to the escalating costs, legal disputes and arguments among the consortium partners (Shell, ENI, Exxon Mobil and Conoco Phillips) who are developing Kashagan. The first phase of the development is likely to produce 370,000 bpd by early 2013. Yet Kashagan, in its second phase, is one of the few fields in the world capable of producing over one million bpd. The potential is real but the timetable is slipping. Rumours abound predicting changes in the consortium and instabilities over the contributions to development costs from the government of Kazakhstan.

Stability is always an issue in Central Asia and the sheer complexity of the pipeline networks which cross so many countries, particularly Russia, serve as a reminder that politics and relations with neigh-bouring states are of crucial importance. But as later chapters of this book show, President Nazarbayev is a foreign policy strategist with a remarkable record of successes in the past twenty years. In oil and gas transportation he is diversifying fast. Although relations with Russia are good, there is no doubt that Kazakhstan wants to be less dependent on pipelines that pass through the territory of its mighty northern neighbour. So it takes what Nazarbayev calls a 'multi-vector approach' to both its foreign policy and its transport policy, linking the two closely together.

What this means in practice is that there are already, or soon will be, oil and gas pipelines between Kazakhstan and China; Kazakhstan and Europe and Kazakhstan to Iran and Turkey. The last two networks will rely heavily on tankers shipping oil to the Western and Southern shores of the Caspian or on new underwater pipelines. There are many technological, environmental and political risk factors in this ambitious strategy, including further wrangling about the legal status of the Caspian Sea.

There are also concerns about contract stability between the government of Kazakhstan and the major operating consortium in the largest fields. In simplified terms, the Kazakhstani negotiators want to improve the local content in these contracts which means what the critics call 'moving the goal posts to increase the rewards for KazMunaiGas'. So far there has been much talking but no real movement. However pressure on the companies is building in areas such as delays and obstacles to the issuing of work permits. As recently as April 2011 The British Ambassador to Kazakhstan, David Moran warned in a speech in Atyrau that in the biggest fields 'all three projects may be in danger of losing momentum to the detriment of both investors and the Government of Kazakhstan'. His views are widely and more outspokenly shared.

No one should ever have expected that oil production in the politically and climatically difficult waters in and around the Caspian would be easy. Yet the story so far is a dream come true for Kazakhstan. Twenty years ago the country had no oil to speak of, no oil industry and few energy prospects. Today it is pumping 1.6 million barrels a day of oil and sitting on recoverable reserves of thirty billion barrels. It also has known gas reserves of 3.3 trillion cubic metres of Natural Gas. Perhaps the most important development of all is that the new energy industries are providing education, training, expertise and jobs for tens of thousands of young Kazakhstanis. The Chevron consortium alone employs an eighty-five per cent Kazakhstani work force in its operations of Tengiz. This desire of the government to develop its own indigenous oil industry at the highest levels of capacity and capability is admirable. Yet it is only one part of a much wider economic strategy for jobs, investment and the Kazakhstanisation of industry which goes far beyond the world of oil and gas.

*   *   *

(III) THE DRIVE TO DIVERSIFICATION
– AGRICULTURE AND MINING

In early 2011 President Nazarbayev made two major speeches focused largely on the country's economic prospects. Oil and gas barely rated a mention in either of them. Since hydrocarbon fuels remain the driving force of growth in the economy, this omission from both the State of the Nation speech to Parliament and the Presidential inauguration address was surprising. The probable explanation was that Nazarbayev is doing his utmost to diversify Kazakhstan's economy into new strategic industries.

The curse of oil has long been a worry to thoughtful Kazakhstanis. Some of Nazarbayev's most far-sighted speeches in the 1990s were sceptical about the predominance of the boom in the Caspian. 'We must not sink our citizens and our economy's competitiveness in oil dollars', he said in 1998, 'we must live and work as though we do not have any oil'.

This was a bold vision but a difficult one. It was partly blown off course by the world recession and global banking crisis of 2008-9. One of the building blocks for the vision, originally called The Fund for Future Generations, now the National Fund, had to be used as a bail-out fund for banks and other troubled industries at the height of the crisis.

Now that the crisis is over and the National Fund has been replenished to a level of $35 billion (with another $33 billion in National

Bank reserves) the country's energy export revenues will be recycled through the fund to the non-oil sectors as the driver of the diversification strategy. But will it work? And if so which are the industries that will benefit? Older sectors of the non-oil economy are likely to be the earliest beneficiaries, particularly agriculture and mining. Kazakhstan has been in both businesses a long time, with deplorable inefficiency in Soviet times but now with a new sense of direction.

Agriculture is booming today. After a collapse in the early 1990s when farmers were having to slaughter their breeding cattle and leave their land derelict, the sector has revived to record levels of production, much assisted by the soaring levels of world food prices and by generous government financing.

'It is not fanciful to say that our agriculture rather than our oil and gas will be the locomotive of Kazakhstan's economy in years to come', says Agriculture Minister Akylbek Kurishbayev,[2] 'already we are one of the world's major exporters of wheat growing eighteen million tons from twenty-two million hectares of wheat fields. Our wheat quality is of such high grade that other countries buy it to mix with their home grown grain. Only Canada can equal us'.

Some of this high productivity is due to a switch by many of Kazakhstan's 155,000 farms and 6,000 agricultural holding companies to US methods and machinery. The same goes for a massive restructuring and expansion of the country's cattle industry.

In the autumn of 2010 over 2,000 Angus and Hereford cattle were flown to Kazakhstan from North Dakota. This airlift was the opening phase of an ambitious project to upgrade the cattle herds of the country. 'We are buying the finest cattle from North Dakota because they have the best breeding stock reared in a harsh climate with extreme weather conditions similar to those of Kazakhstan', says Asylzhan Mamytbekhov,[3] the chairman of KazAgro, the country's main agricultural development and export corporation. His objective is to boost high quality beef production to around 580,000 tons a year by 2015. This would represent a thirty-four per cent increase in current output. Similar production leaps are being aimed for in sheep and poultry, again using the latest US scientific methods in nutrition, veterinary care and animal husbandry.

Kazakhs, with their nomad heritage, know their meat and cattle rearing better than any other nation in Asia. But they fell badly behind the curve of scientific knowledge during the last decade of Soviet rule and in the first fifteen years of independence. Now they are back in the cattle export business at the highest level of quality, largely thanks to specialist American know how. The Kazakhstan government is playing a key part in this upgrading of the herds providing farmers with $10 billion of soft loans and credits. In his 2011 State of the Nation speech President Nazarbayev claimed that the initiative would create more than 20,000 jobs in the countryside and provide a source of income for over 100,000 rural villagers.

Behind the drive to expand the nation's agriculture lie two traditional Kazakh passions – love of horses and enjoyment of meat eating. The horse is a symbol of the nation's nomadic history which still flourishes today. Modern Kazakhstan is home to 1.2 million horses, a fifty per cent increase from Soviet times, most of them running wild in huge herds until slaughtered for consumption. Kazakhs are said to be the world's largest eaters of horse meat and all other kinds of meat.

There is an apocryphal story about this national characteristic which revolves around a UN survey into which country consumes the most meat. Kazakhstan came second. The Kazakhs were upset and lodged an official protest, demanding to know who had overtaken them in the No 1 slot. Some wag in the UN's research department replied 'the wolves'.

Behind the joke lies the truth that this is a country where the meat culture is seriously important. It is another reason why the government's emphasis on reviving the livestock industry is a popular element in the diversification strategy.

Mining has also been part of Kazakhstan's culture for a long time. Throughout most of the twentieth century, the republic's potential as a quarry for the rest of the Soviet Union was exploited to the full but inefficiently and with scant regard for those working in the mines. As a young politician in the early 1970's Nazarbayev made a name for himself by championing the cause of improving conditions for the coal miners of Karaganda. He was a lonely voice on the issue, possibly because he had seen appalling industrial accidents as a steel worker. Today in the mines both the safety and productivity are far better. Kazakhstan is one of the world's top ten coal producing countries. Its fifty-three pits, fifteen of them in the Karaganda coal basin, have an annual output of over one hundred and ten million tons. Most of this output is exported to Russia which uses it as cheap fuel for its power plants in Siberia and the Urals.

Since independence Kazakhstan has expanded its mining industry with considerable backing from foreign investors. Aside from the state owned uranium industry (reported separately in Chapter 5) there are huge deposits of copper, iron ore, chrome, zinc, lead, manganese, silver, gold, rare earths and the complete periodic spectrum of minerals. Kazakhstan is the sixth richest country in the world measured in natural mineral wealth, with the added advantage that most of its deposits often lie near the surface and can be extracted using cheap open-cast mining methods.

Two of Kazakhstan's biggest mining companies, Kazakhmys and Eurasian Natural Resources Corporation, pioneered the listing of their shares by IPO on the London Stock Exchange. These multi-million dollar placings, which immediately raised the profile of Kazakhstan throughout the global financial community, were approved and encouraged by President Nazarbayev. He gave his blessing to this initiative partly to carry his domestic free market philosophy on to the international stage of world stock markets and partly to introduce full accounting transparency into the country. For the IPOs introduced the disciplines and standards of public company accounts verified by international firms of accountants. This was a step change for the leaders of the business community in Kazakhstan.

For some of those leaders the step has proved too large. In recent months the Eurasian National Resources Corporation (ENRC) has been plagued by boardroom rows, a plummeting share price, diktats from its major Kazakh shareholders, and a breakdown of the normal rules of corporate governance. One of the international non-executive directors who quit ENRC's board in the middle of these upheavals disturbingly described the company as "more Soviet than City".

By contrast the more acceptable face of capitalism in Kazakhstan is 49 year old Vladimir Kim, Chairman, chief executive and principal shareholder of Kazakhmys, which is now a FTSE 100 company, and one of the world's leading copper producers. Vladimir Kim is reported by Forbes Magazine to be the richest billionaire in Kazakhstan with a net worth of $4.7 billion. I found him in an ebullient mood when I interviewed him in his palatial office in the Kazakhmys headquarters building in downtown Almaty in January 2011.

'This is a young country and a young economy but look how well we are doing!' he said, 'our shares have gone up from $3 to $21 in the past five years and our growth in export markets is soaring. Of course the tremendous demand for copper from China has helped us but another of our strengths is the people who work for us. This is a country of equality in opportunities. Look at me! I am a citizen of Kazakhstan but I was born a Korean. Talent and hard work can get you anywhere here. The brains of the country are even more important than the raw materials of the country. But we do have to develop new expertise beyond mining our natural resources. This is the reason I have now started Kazakhmys Engineering, a subsidiary that will build machinery and manufacture the goods we now import'.

I asked Vladimir Kim what his subsidiary could make that can compete with China in price. 'We will be smarter than the Chinese!' he replied, 'we start with the great advantage of having our own cheap raw materials. Now, thanks to the Customs Union President Nazarbayev has negotiated with Russia, we have a new home market of almost 200 million people. We can certainly be competitive with Russian manufacturing industry in products we now import from them – simple engineering equipment like snow ploughs or power generators. This is where we will begin'.

The beginnings have so far been slow. Kazakhmys is good at producing copper but bad at adding value to the raw material it extracts from its mines. 'President Nazarbayev keeps urging us to do more manufacturing but the problem is that the profit margins from mining are far greater. How do I explain that to my shareholders?' Says Mr Kim in a tone that sounds apologetic. As we are leaving his huge office, full of modernistic furniture and state of the art technology I ask him if anything in the room is manufactured domestically?'Nothing yet', he replies. This lack of 'Made in Kazakhstan' products is the economy's greatest weakness. Can it be turned around into a national opportunity?

*   *   *

(IV) THE DRIVE TO DIVERSIFICATION – ENTREPRENEURS, SMES AND MANUFACTURING INDUSTRY

If political speeches could shape an economy, Kazakhstan would be doing well in its drive to diversification. President Nazarbayev is an eloquent orator on the subject of strategic plans for the next decade. They include goals such as 'creating an entrepreneurial class', forecasts such as 'the share of small and medium sized enterprises (SMEs) in the country's GDP will be at least forty per cent by 2020'; and targets like 'we will proceed with a search for one hundred absolute innovations and focus on the implementation of the ten most promising of them'. The President's overall goal for his government is to develop Kazakhstan's business environment so that it becomes one of the world's top fifty economies for competitiveness.

These are serious objectives and significant progress towards them has been made. In 2011 The World Bank's *Doing Business* report awarded Kazakhstan the No 1 position as the world's most reformed business economy. Prime Minister Karim Massimov told this author 'this is my proudest achievement'. He can point to some encouraging results. Corporation tax has been reduced to twenty per cent and will fall to fifteen per cent by 2012. Investor protection laws and accountancy transparency regulations have been strengthened. The cost (expressed as a percentage of per capita income) and the minimum capital required to start a new business are now significantly lower than the OECD and emerging European regional averages.

Yet there are problems for business start ups as well, among them excessive red tape, bureaucratic delays, corruption and a shortage of available credit from banks. This does not deter big foreign investors but it does put off smaller potential providers of overseas capital. So the notion that Kazakhstan is fertile territory for SME's entrepreneurship and manufacturing industry is tomorrow's dream rather than today's reality. Nevertheless there are some indications that the tide may be turning in the direction signposted by Nazarbayev's speeches. I identified some of them during a discussion I had with the Almaty Chapter of the Young President's Organization of YPO.

The YPO is one of the world's most influential groups of successful young business executives. It has 17,000 members in 120 countries. All have to be under forty-five, running or owning a company that has annual sales in excess of $10 million and employing a staff of at least fifty people. The YPO of Almaty is the organization's newest chapter, founded in 2010. There are eleven business proprietors or CEOs in the city who have so far qualified to join as full YPO members. Their Chairman is Nurlan Kapparov, a Harvard graduate and a former Vice Minister for oil and energy who now owns a group of companies, Lancaster Holdings, with interests ranging from solar power to financial services. He and another six YPO colleagues met me over tea in a fashionable Almaty Bar. Their views on the outlook for their businesses were positive but not as optimistic as the opinions of the government ministers who preside over the economy.

'You have to remember that this is still only a partly free and partly deregulated economy from the point of view of an entrepreneur', said Nurlan Kapparov, 'over a third of the business world is controlled by the state holding company Samruk and another third or more is controlled by major foreign investors in natural resources such as Chevron, BG, or ENI. When you look at the last third of the business environment it is quite weak. Less than ten per cent of the economy consists of SMEs. They often lack a skilled workforce. The number of entrepreneurs is not growing at anything like the rate the President is hoping for. So this part of our economy is not moving forward fast enough due to our structural problems, many of which are a legacy from the Soviet era'.

The YPO members I met broadly agreed with this assessment. But they did identify six 'niche areas' where it is possible to start and run a successful entrepreneurial business. These were:Mining; Agriculture and food distribution; Transportation; Retail; Construction and the Services sector including tourism and finance. Even these niches are subject to various forms of bureaucratic control such as licensing procedures.

'You can do well out of mining but you have to stick pretty close to the government', says Erlan Sagadiev, CEO of Frontier Mining whose interests include gold and copper mines in eastern Kazakhstan, 'this is a workable environment but it is still held back by bureaucratic bottlenecks'.

Among the few completely deregulated sectors of business are real estate, tourism and the processing of agricultural products. A YPO who specializes in all three of them is Erlan Kozhasbay who also chairs the national chamber of commerce. He made his first money by creating a network of gas stations in Almaty in 1997. Then after a spell as Deputy CEO of the national railways he went to study in France and then at Moscow State University where he obtained an MBA. Returning to Kazakhstan in 2005 he entered the world of real estate development by building a 60,000 square metre shopping mall in downtown Almaty. He suffered in but survived the property crash of 2007–9. 'The banks were badly scarred and they squeezed many of their customers during the crisis. Even now bank lending has not really recovered', says Kozhasbay, 'but I built and now manage three hotels and a mall so I am succeeding in my core business of real estate. My next business move will be into the processing of agricultural products. This has a bright future and the government is likely to be willing to make credit available for new food processing factories'.

The one area of doubt among the YPO members concerns the future of manufacturing industry. Their pessimism was confirmed in my later interview with Kadyr Baykenov, Chairman of the Union of Engineering Companies Association which has over two hundred member firms.

'I am sorry to say that our manufacturing and engineering companies are not competitive in world markets', said Chairman Baykenov, 'the prestige of this sector has been low for a long time. The average age of engineers in Kazakhstan is fifty-five. We are doing our best to train new engineers but it is difficult. The recession hit us hard. The government produced funds to help SMEs to survive but eighty-five per cent of the money ended up in the services sector and only fifteen per cent was allocated to companies which actually make something'.

Asked what Kazakhstan's successful companies in the engineering field were manufacturing Mr Baykenov's answer was a gloomy one. 'If you are talking about companies which design and build products from start to finish we do not have that here', he said 'we do make some basic industrial supplies for the energy industry such as plastic and polystyrene materials but finished goods are almost all imported from China, Russia and Ukraine. We badly need to develop our own machine tool industry as a starting point here, but so far we have been blocked by Russia refusing to sell us the basic jigs and kit material'.

There are a handful of high profile projects which may help to overcome such obstacles. These include a nuclear fuel rod production plant at Ulba, and a railway locomotives factory in Astana. Both are joint ventures with major international corporations, respectively Areva of France and General Electric of the USA. However there are doubts whether such projects are merely assembly lines rather than true manufacturing plants.

The present weakness of the manufacturing and engineering sectors is the Achilles heel of Kazakhstan's grand strategy for a diversified economy. It is hard to see how this problem can be overcome when the country has China as a next door neighbour and an overpowering source of cheap imports. However, growth itself will not be held back because the prospects for natural resources are so strong. But these need capital investment on a huge scale which in turn need foreign investors. This is an area in which Kazakhstan has been enjoying considerable success for some years.

*   *   *

(V) FOREIGN INVESTMENT

Kazakhstan depends on Foreign Investment and has been successful at attracting it. Since independence there has been an inflow of overseas capital in excess of $122 billion, of which $70 billion has been invested in the last five years. However, almost all of these funds have been directed towards the natural resources sector with heavy weights towards the oil industry.

The legal and political framework for encouraging foreign investments is favourable but the system is still overburdened by red tape and excessive bureaucracy, particularly at local level. However, in 2011 new legislation has been passed by Parliament to streamline what is known as the 'permitting' process of permits and documents that have to be obtained by a foreign investor when starting a new business. The new laws are expected to decrease documentation requirements by as much as thirty per cent.

At the highest level of decision making, the encouragement of FDI (Foreign Direct Investment) works well because both President Nazarbayev and Prime Minister Massimov take a hands on approach to major investors. In the early years of bringing business pioneers to Kazakhstan, such as Chevron and Philip Morris, Nazarbayev negotiated the terms of their agreements with his government personally. He still stays close to the country's largest overseas investors by one-on-one meetings and through the mechanism of the Foreign Investors Council (FIC).

I attended one of the bi-annual meetings of FIC in 2008. It was held in Atyrau, the oil capital of the Caspian region. The proceedings, although advisory in nature, were impressive because of the quality of direct dialogue between government ministers and foreign investors. Even more impressive was President Nazarbayev's attentive presence at most sessions of the conference.

The Atyrau FIC meeting was attended by over seventy Chairmen, CEOs or their equivalents from global corporations including Arcelor-Mittal, JP Morgan, BG Group, Chevron, Royal Dutch Shell, Deutsche Bank, Lukoil, Exxonmobile, Philip Morris, ABN Aurora Bank, Price

Waterhouse Coopers and many others. This particular agenda was focused on the development of a more efficient power generation industry for Kazakhstan. With most of his cabinet in attendance, Nazarbayev listened for several hours to a discussion of detailed issues ranging from the practical technicalities of modernising the country's electricity grid to government grants and incentives for companies willing to invest in the new power generating infrastructure. It is hard to think of any other modern state in which the President gets down to such a level of practical co-operation with foreign investors.

In the margins of the public sessions, Nazarbayev had private bilateral meetings with overseas corporate leaders such as Lakshmi Mittal of Arcelor Mittal; Lord Renwick of JP Morgan; Vagit Alekperov of Lukoil; Bill O'Reilly of Chevron; Leonard Blavatnik of Access Industries and Sir Richard Evans the former supremo of BAE Systems who now plays a key role within the national state holding company Samruk-Kazyna.

Nazarbayev the politician loves announcing good economic news to his countrymen and to the foreign investors in Kazakhstan. So on the final evening of the FIC, after feasting his guests on mountainous platefuls of Beluga caviar which came straight from the roes of freshly caught Caspian sturgeon laid out like corpses for dissection on nearby serving tables, Nazarbayev toasted the major new projects which foreign investors were bringing to his country. With the panache of a conjuror producing rabbits out of a top hat, the President described the Arcelor Mittal investment to expand production at the Karaganda Steel Plant from six billion to ten million tonnes a year; as he outlined the second phase of production at Tengiz and the prospects for the Kashagan field; and as he announced the new petrochemical plants to be built near Kuryk. Some of these projects have come to fulfilment already. Others, such as the development of Kashagan, are in danger of losing momentum because of technical difficulties and lack of contract stability. All will probably need more hands-on attention from the President before the projected results are delivered. Nazarbayev is good at this level of personalized economic diplomacy. One of his more spectacular recent coups was to persuade the Abu Dhabi Investment Authority (ADIA) to invest over $1 billion in a huge real estate development in Astana known at Abu Dhabi Plaza.

Foreign investor stability, like the stability of the country itself, comes back in the end to President Nazarbayev. The 2011 election has delivered strong political foundations on which to base further economic momentum. But this in turn depends, in a mixed economy like Kazakhstan, on the relationship between the private and public sectors, with particular focus on the state holding company Samruk-Kazyna and its new chairman Timur Kulibayev.

*   *   *

(VI) SAMRUK-KAZYNA AND TIMUR KULIBAYEV

When President Nazarbayev re-shuffled his cabinet and made strategic changes among senior government officials following the election of April 2011, one new appointment caused a flurry of domestic and international media interest. This was the choice of Timur Kulibayev to head the country's Sovereign wealth fund, Samruk-Kazyna.

Because Kulibayev is the President's son-in-law, his promotion caused cynical comments on some blogs suggesting that this was the first move signposting a dynastic political succession in Kazakhstan. This is over-excitable speculation. In terms of ability, Kulibayev has long been one of the most effective and successful business leaders in the country. No doubt his family connections have helped his rise. Yet informed observers say that on his own merits he is the right man to take on the huge task of running Samruk-Kazyna and privatizing significant parts of it. So who is Timur Kulibayev and what are the challenges he faces in his new job?

In the monochrome world of Kazakhstan's state controlled industries Kulibayev stands out as a colourful figure. A graduate in economics from Moscow State University in 1988, his early business career in the years after independence was notable for successful entrepreneurial deal making. After marriage to the President's daughter, Dinara Nazarbayeva, his profile and his profits increased. Forbes Magazine recently estimated his net worth to be in excess of $2 billion.

Charming and charismatic in his personality, Timur Kulibayev has stayed in the spotlight of domestic and international media attention. He is a businessman rather than a politician, so the blogger's suggestions that he might one day succeed his father-in-law as President seem prematurely wide of the mark.

Western newspapers have stereotyped Kulibayev as a playboy. He has been linked to a London-based Kazakh socialite Goga Ashkenazi and to unconfirmed reports that through her he paid £15 million sterling (£3million more than the asking price) to buy the Duke of York's house in Sunninghill, Berkshire. Although such rumours circulate at cocktail parties, in boardrooms and business offices Kulibayev is seen as a heavyweight. In his new job he will have to do some heavy lifting for his country as he faces up to the challenges of reforming the energy sector and in privatizing parts of Samruk-Kazyna's portfolio of state industries.

'Timur Kulibayev is one of the few Kazakh leaders who knows how business works and how to deliver results' says Sir Richard Evans, the former Chairman and CEO of British Aerospace who now sits on the Samruk-Kazyna board. 'If he can't do the job of running the country's energy industries and launching the privatization program through IPOs, no-one can do it. He has the ability, the clout and the connections. If he dedicates himself to the big picture and doesn't get distracted, he will make a great success of it.'

The privatisation programme, called 'The Peoples' IPOs' (International Public Offering) has enormous potential. It offers Kazakhstan its best chance of raising capital and entering the international debt market. Inspired by Margaret Thatcher's privatisation policies of the 1980s in Britain, Samruk-Kazyna owns assets which many local and overseas investors will want to buy. Starting with the country's primary resource based industries such as KazMunaiGas, there is a profitable portfolio of Samruk companies which could benefit by encouraging the participation of private shareholders. They include Kazakhstan Electricity Grid Operating Company (KEGOC); the national network of post offices KAZPOST; the national airline AIR ASTANA and the national telephone company KAZAKHTELEKOM. There are over 400 Samruk owned joint stock companies in areas such as civil engineering, mining, oil exploration and railways which could successfully be opened up to part or full ownership by the private sector. In total Samruk-Kazyna owns thirty-eight per cent of the nation's entire economic assets, so the scope for selective sales by IPO is massive.

The process of privatisation by 'People's IPOs' is at present opaque. Timur Kulibayev and Prime Minister Massimov have announced a selected group of IPO consultants including Citibank, UBS and PriceWaterhouseCoopers. There are suggestions that local pension funds and local investors (buying through post offices) will be given first priority. Major international institutions will also be able to participate. On the domestic front it is suggested that a national investor publicity campaign will have to be launched. The consultants are digging out the advertisements of the British government's privatizations campaign of the 1980s, including those featuring 'Sid' – the working man who bought British Gas shares.

All this suggests an exciting ride for Kazakhstan and Timur Kulibayev. If he sorts out the problems of Kashagan and other Caspian oil fields the national revenues will double by 2015. If he gets privatization right, the IPOs could be a major catalyst for economic liberalization, modernization, transparency and growth. If both policies succeed the economy of Kazakhstan will be poised for its greatest leap forward since independence twenty years ago.

8

The Dragon, the Bear and the Unstable Neighbourhood

(I) GEOGRAPHY AND NUMBERS

Kazakhstan has a small population inhabiting a colossal land mass. A glance at the map is enough to indicate the scale of its problems and opportunities. Its northern border with Russia (6,847 kilometres) is longer than that of Canada's land border with the United States. Five times bigger than Texas, it is the ninth largest country in the world, beginning on the shores of the Caspian sea where Asia meets Europe and ending on its 1,533 kilometre frontier with Western China.

Living alongside these giants was historically a cause of fear, warfare and subjugation for the Kazakh nomads. Those days are gone. But even in the twenty-first century where borders are secured by international law and where military invasion is unthinkable, some traces of the country's ancestral anxieties are bound to remain.

Kazakhstan's 16 million people, owners of some of the world's richest natural resources, are next door neighbours to 1.3 billion Chinese and 140 million Russians. Looking around the rest of the region, Central Asia is a cockpit of present or potential chaos. Afghanistan, Uzbekistan, Kyrgyzstan, Tajikistan and Turkmenistan are seething sources of war, civil unrest, tribal conflicts and Islamist extremism.

Compared to the rest of the stans, sometimes collectively dismissed as 'Trashcanistan', Kazakhstan has emerged as a beacon of economic progress and political stability. 'But for how long?' ask the pessimists. The optimists reply that it will survive and prosper. This is because its 'multi-vector foreign policy' has had the strategic objective of building strong foundations in its relationships with the West, China and Russia. On account of their immediate proximity, it is the last two which will have most sway over the long term prospects for Kazakhstan's future.

* * *

(II) RIDING THE DRAGON

In February 2011, a China-Kazakhstan summit took place in Beijing. The diplomatic atmospherics were unusually warm and the economic results were unexpectedly large.

The first signal of special treatment was an unexpected invitation from PRC Chairman Hu Jintao for President Nazarbayev to come and dine with him informally on the eve of the summit. The two leaders, who have known each other well for over a decade, wore open-neck shirts and evidently enjoyed their relaxed evening at the Chairman's home. The warmth of Hu Jintao's toast surprised everyone present. 'China has no better friend in today's world than Kazakhstan', he declared.

A national leader is not on oath in the setting of a private dinner to welcome a visiting head of state. Yet even after allowing for a touch of hyperbole and for the realpolitik fact that China has national interests rather than friendships, the Chairman's words rang true. On the hyper-sensitive measuring scale of Beijing's international diplomacy, Kazakhstan probably is the Middle Kingdom's most compliant and least complaining neighbour.

As the official agenda of the summit got underway, the atmospherics of good neighbourliness turned into a bonanza of loans, grants and investment projects for the benefit of Kazakhstan. 'The deals exceeded all expectations' said Kuanish Sultanov, a former Kazakh Ambassador to Beijing (1995–2001), 'our trade with China is now over $20 billion a year compared to $1 billion a year ten years ago. At the summit we received loans and credits worth $5 billion with which we are developing projects such as an expansion of the oil and gas pipelines between our countries; a creation of a Europe-China highway which runs for 2,900 kilometres across Kazakhstan's territory; the creation of a free trade zone at the new border crossing of Khorgos and the establishment of a Chinese-Kazakh Supercomputer Centre in Astana. We also received big export orders for uranium pellets, oil, minerals and agricultural commodities'.

The most symbolically important project was China's offer to build a new high speed train link between Astana and Almaty. On the third day of the state visit President Nazarbayev travelled on the showpiece CHR3 train from Beijing South railway station to Tianjin. According to his awestruck fellow passenger, Senator Sultanov, 'this new technology railway line is far superior to the Japanese bullet train. Our journey covered 150 kilometres in twenty-seven minutes. At one point we reached 394 kilometres per hour and you couldn't even see the glasses on the table in front of us quiver'.

In Soviet times this rail journey took over twenty-four hours. In 2004 a Spanish built train halved the travelling time to twelve hours. Within three years China's state of the art rail technology should create a 350 kmph express train covering the 1,200 kilometre distance between Kazakhstan's first and second cities in less than four hours. There may now be delays in this timetable following questions about China's rail technology that have been raised by the crash of a high speed train near Beijiing in the summer of 2011. But with so much national pride now at stake over this project it seems likely that Chinese built trains will soon be running swiftly and safely between Almaty and Astana.

When Kazakhstan became an independent country twenty years ago nobody knew how Beijing would treat its new neighbour. The signs were not encouraging. In addition to the historical enmity between Kazakhs and Chinese caused by centuries of Junghar wars, there were troublesome twentieth century frictions. Beijing's policy seemed to be not to agree borders with any of its neighbouring former republics of the Soviet Union. Some Mandarin maps even showed large regions of Kazakhstan, including Lake Balkhash, as Chinese territory. So claims and counter claims about disputed frontiers were a neuralgic issue, as were water rights and the poor treatment of the 1–2 million Kazakhs living in Xinjiang province.

The problems were overcome because both countries were guided in the mid 1990s by national leaders who spoke a common language, shared a common vision and were determined to find solutions swiftly. The Chairman of the Peoples Republic of China, Jiang Zemin, spoke fluent Russian as a result of having worked on the assembly line of a Soviet automobile factory in Gorky. President Nazarbayev had acquired his Russian fluency as a blast furnace operator in a Soviet steelworks. Dispensing with interpreters at their summit meetings the two leaders were able to drop diplomatic formalities and to discover that they had an instinctive rapport for finding their way round the longstanding obstacles to good Sino-Kazakh relations. At one point in the difficult negotiations on disputed border claims, Jiang Zemin said with unusual candour to Nazarbayev, 'We must settle these border issues now, while we are both in charge. One day in the future a new generation may come to lead China who I am not so sure will be so eager to reach an agreement'. With such a warning ringing in his ear Nazarbayev needed no urging to achieve an accord. The territorial issues were solved shortly afterwards in a deal which gave fifty-three per cent of the contested regions to Kazakhstan and forty-seven per cent to China. The agreement was subsequently ratified as a treaty by both national parliaments. This was an historic breakthrough. After centuries of wars, invasions, skirmishes and clashes in the disputed areas, Kazakhstan and China had a judicially ratified border from 1998 onwards.

There are still some sensitive cross-border issues which need careful handling. At one point in the 2011 summit the head of Kazakhstan's Security Service, or KNB, Nurtai Abikayev, held a secret bilateral with his opposite number, the chief of China's national security bureau. 'We had a remarkably fruitful meeting as we discussed in detail the problem of the three evils – terrorism, separatism and extremism' said Abikayev in an interview with this author after the summit. 'China and Kazakhstan are united on these issues, particularly in regard to the Uigur separatists. As a sign of our unity my colleague, the head of China's national security bureau, who has never travelled outside his country's borders before, accepted my invitation to make an official visit to Astana later this year. In the security world, this level of face to face co-operation, which includes co-operation with the head of Russia's security intelligence service, is a new breakthrough.'

Breakthrough was a word much used by the Kazakh delegation to Beijing in February 2011, but credit for the original groundbreaking border agreements go to Nazarbayev and to his then Foreign Minister who conducted the detailed bilateral negotiations – Kassym-Jomart Tokayev.

Tokayev had been trained for a career in diplomacy with China at the Moscow State Institute of Foreign Relations after winning a scholarship there from his high school in Almaty. Following his intensive tuition in the Chinese language, Tokayev was assigned to the Far Eastern division of the Soviet Foreign Ministry and served long tours of duty in the embassy in Beijing during the 1980s. This professional experience proved invaluable to his native country Kazakhstan in the decade after independence when negotiations with China were one of the highest priorities of the new nation's diplomatic effort. Tokayev, who is now the Under Secretary General of the United Nations in Geneva, recalls the domestic reaction to his success in the border negotiations with wry humour:

'Naturally in the Foreign Ministry we were delighted to have settled our borders with China. It was undoubtedly the right strategic decision by President Nazarbayev. But back at home there were many self-styled experts who thought they knew better. So they raised their voices to say that we had given far too much away and that the Chinese had got the better of us. These voices were wrong but they made a lot of noise'.

The noises of anti-China hostility still make themselves heard in today's Kazakhstan. At the time of the 2011 Beijing summit Almaty's opposition newspapers published fantastic conspiracy theories whose gist was that Nazarbayev had secretly sold large tracts of territory in the north west of the country to the land hungry PRC. These stories had their origin in a rash off-the-cuff statement made in 2009 by the President when speaking at a Foreign Investors Conference in Almaty. In an ill-judged aside, Nazarbayev had appeared to suggest that Kazakhstan might be willing to lease up to a million hectares of its unused agricultural land to Chinese farmers.

Within two days of this comment becoming public, demonstrators were marching in protest against it outside the Chinese Consulate in Almaty. The government of Kazakhstan beat a hasty retreat, issuing statements of 'clarification'. But the air had evidently not quite cleared enough. So the rumours re-surfaced in February 2011 at the instigation of the President's trouble-making son-in-law in exile, Rakhat Aliyev. Since he is notorious in Kazakhstan for his malevolent unreliability, Aliyev's stirrings found few takers. But the fact that such rumours gained even the slightest credence illustrates the uncomfortable truth that many Kazakhs have a deep seated fear of eventual Chinese colonization.

These fears are rooted in economic and population figures. Within the next five years China will easily overtake Russia as Kazakhstan's largest export market. Already it is the banks and finance houses of Beijing which are supplying the lion's share of foreign credit for every kind of natural resources deal from agriculture to zircon mining. But these great leaps forward in trade are not being accompanied by friendship. In an effort to change such attitudes Nazarbayev and his ministers are doing their best to improve Sino-Kazakh understanding. Over two thousand Kazakhstani students now receive their higher education in the PRC. A new university-level Institute in Chinese studies will soon be opening in Astana. But despite such initiatives the mood of the general public remains stubbornly hostile to the manifest expansion of all things Chinese in Kazakhstan, from the illegal immigrants who surface in Almaty's flea markets to the growing number of Chinese-owned businesses.

These trends are irreversible. All that even the most ardent Kazakh nationalists can do is to grumble about them, often with gallows humour. 'If you are planning to leave this country – learn English. If you want to stay here – learn Chinese', is one local joke. Another describes a visitor from Beijing asking, 'How big is your population?' '16 million people', replies a proud Kazakh. 'So, all your citizens must recognize each other personally then', is the Chinese visitor's condescending response.

Whether in fun or in fear, negative responses by Kazakh nationalists to China's overpowering economic and population power are pointless. Nazarbayev has made the right policy decisions to embrace the hand of self-interested friendship offered by Beijing. But he is balancing his embrace by simultaneously developing good relations with the West, by raising Kazakhstan's profile in the international community and above all the maintaining his country's primary friendship with Russia.

* * *

(III) COMING TO NEW TERMS WITH RUSSIA

Kazakhstanis get along much better with the Russians than they do with the Chinese. This is because relations with their northern neighbour, although often difficult, have deeper roots. To a considerable extent the two countries share a common language, culture and history. The Soviet heritage, brutally imposed though it was for much of the twentieth century, also brought great benefits to Kazakhstan. Many of the country's best schools, technical colleges, scientific institutes and cultural activities owe their quality to standards set in Moscow. Most important of all, twenty-three per cent of Kazakhstan's population are ethnic Russians. Some of them have lived in the country for three or four generations and have risen to prominent positions. For example the Governor of the Central Bank, Grigory Marchenko, comes from a Russian family who have been in Kazakhstan for 108 years.

Such links make the relationship workable because of mutual understanding. Yet shadows of suspicion continue. A further complicating factor is that the old Russian condescension is starting to be eroded by new Kazakhstani achievement. Few Muscovites yet admit it, but there is more enlightened progress in Almaty and Astana than in most Russian cities. Times are changing – and in Kazakhstan's favour.

In the immediate years after independence, Kazakhstan was roughly treated by the Russian governing elite. In the middle of their own political chaos, they exploited their southern neighbour as if it was a backward colony. The betrayals by Moscow over currency arrangements, oil pipeline deals and broken promises on tariffs and trade brought Kazakh negotiators to the brink of despair.

Yet even at the worst moments, the highest channels of politics kept open. The Kremlin never forgot that Kazakhstan was the last republic to leave the Soviet Union in December 1991. It always remembered that Nazarbayev had been a formidably effective Politburo member even though it became increasingly obvious that he was ditching communism and promoting nationalism in the last years of the Gorbachev era. This bedrock of respect for the Kazakh leader manifested itself most clearly in the relationship between Boris Yeltsin and Nursultan Nazarbayev. The dealings between the two Presidents were extensive and usually had results which were favourable to Kazakhstan.

The old Russian saying 'made from the same dough' was particularly applicable to Nazarbayev and Yeltsin. It goes some way to explaining their personal rapport, their rough and ready styles of communicating and their ability to reach difficult but important agreements at their summits in areas that had been frustrated by years of stalemate among their sub-ordinates. Both men were outsiders who had come up the hard way in political life. Nurtured by their strong roots from rural backgrounds they were influenced more by inner instincts than by outer pressures. They indulged in much showmanship, wrapping up their diplomatic bargaining with humour and heavy vodka toasting. But they cut big deals, believing that prolonged confrontation over issues such as nuclear warheads, Caspian oil or the Baikonur cosmodrome for space launches was never going to be in the national interest of either country.

When the era of Boris Yeltsin was replaced by the presidencies of Vladimir Putin and Dmitri Medvedev, Kazakhstan-Russian relations became more professional. There were no more episodes of napkin diplomacy (see Chapter 8) or nocturnal duets over multiple vodka shots. But the co-operation at head of state level intensified. It may even be true, as both Putin and Medvedev have claimed, that Astana is their favourite foreign capital.

There are some interesting fresh angles on the steadily improving attitudes between the two countries. First, there is much less anxiety on the Kazakh side of the relationship. They may still feel unequal but they are no longer fearful. Two decades ago when Aleksandr Solzhenitsyn published a pamphlet calling for northern regions of Kazakhstan to be taken back by Russia, it caused a storm of protest demonstrations in the streets of Almaty because the threat seemed real. Today such a suggestion would be dismissed as a minor academic controversy. The stability and prosperity of Kazakhstan has given the country a new self confidence.

Secondly, the novelty in the relationship is coming largely from the Kazakh side. The 2008-9 global banking crisis was handled much more effectively and innovatively in Astana than it was in Moscow. Crime and corruption problems are troublesome to both nations but they are far worse in Russia. Neither Putin nor Nazarbayev are regarded as blue eyed boys of the international human rights scene. But the Kazakh leader does not imprison his political opponents on trumped up charges. He is fighting corruption with growing seriousness. He has relaxed some media freedoms. And he allows independent international observers to monitor and criticize his elections whereas Russia's leaders deride and ban such 'western meddlers' from theirs.

Thanks to a recently signed customs union between the two countries and neighbouring Belarus, trade and travel arrangements are improving. Passengers arriving from Kazakhstan at Moscow airport no longer have their bags searched. Kazakh exporters now have access to a much larger tariff-free home market of 170 million people. In business matters such as the introduction of best European Union practices to accountancy, professional standards, legal procedures and economic transparency it is Kazakhstan which is setting the pace of twenty-first century modernization. In comparison Russia looks sluggish and sclerotic.

A third new ingredient in the relationship between the two neighbours is the changing attitude towards national loyalty among the large number of ethnic Russians who are permanent residents of Kazakhstan. These 4 million expatriates were uneasy citizens of the new nation in the first decade of independence. They instinctively felt tied to Mother Russia by an umbilical cord of language and heritage. They disliked the idea of life without the Soviet Union. They feared that they would be the victims of discrimination by the Kazakh majority. So they welcomed the laws and speeches coming out of the Kremlin in the early 1990s which asserted that they and all other native Russians living in former Soviet Republics would have their rights protected by Moscow. Even if this rhetoric ran ahead of the reality, it was reassuring to the anxious Russians of Kazakhstan.

There is now a subtle shift in such attitudes. Reassurance is becoming more local. So is national identity. The worries about discrimination are fading away. The ethnic Russians of Kazakhstan may not yet feel completely at home in Astana or Almaty, but now they do not fit comfortably in Moscow or St Petersburg either. The rise of a younger generation, the increase in intermarriage and the success of Kazakhstan's efforts at nation building are all having their effect. This is a society in transition.

Many Kazakhs tell stories of ethnic Russians who proclaim (sometimes in television interviews) their feelings of truly belonging to their new homeland. Such declarations are usually made by young people under twenty-five. They seem to be a genuine manifestation of the country's drive towards inclusiveness which now embraces over 138 original nationalities in modern Kazakhstan. Even if the ethnic Russians are the slowest element in the melting pot to melt, they are moving and changing.

Unfortunately, some people never change. There is still a dark side to this relationship. Some Russians sneer openly at 'the dirty nomads' who are becoming so annoyingly rich on their doorstep. There have been nasty episodes of young Kazakhs getting beaten up by skinheads when visiting Russian cities. These racially motivated attacks went noticeably uncondemned by senior Kremlin politicians to the dismay of their opposite numbers in Kazakhstan. So at gut or street level there may still be much to worry about.

Yet for all the qualifications and hesitations, Russia and Kazakhstan have a stable and subtly evolving relationship. Although they dare not boast about it, the nimbler and younger Kazakhs are catching up with the plodding old Bear. Watch this space!

* * *

(IV) INSTABILITY IN THE BACKYARD

Central Asia is a dangerous place, and an important geopolitical cross-roads. Kazakhstan is at the heart of it. In addition to its contiguity with

Europe to the West, Russia to the North and China to the East, the country has the lion's share of the oil rich Caspian sea and is surrounded by a neighbourhood of volatile Stans.

The most difficult immediate neighbour is Uzbekistan. Its twenty-eight million people live under a brutal dictatorship which bears little comparison to Kazakhstan's benevolent autocracy. Uzbeks are poor, for half of them live on less than $1.25 a day. They are oppressed, according to reports from international bodies, by one of the world's worst regimes which carried out wide-scale violation of virtually all basic human rights including torture, arbitrary imprisonment and harsh restrictions on free speech and free association.

Despite the huge disparity in economic and political progress between the two countries since they both left the Soviet Union in 1991, Uzbeks tend to look down on Kazakhs. The basis for this feeling of superiority is that Uzbekistan's principal cities such as Tashkent, Bukhara and Samarkand were founded by cultured and civilized settlers brought in by the fourteenth century conqueror Tamerlane while the Kazakhs remained primitive nomads.

A more contemporary cause of friction is that the President of Uzbekistan is hostile to and jealous of the President of Kazakhstan. This personalized and at times almost unbalanced animosity from the Uzbek leader sours many of the political and diplomatic dealings in the region. To give one recent example, Uzbekistan was the only one of the OSCE's fifty-six member states who opposed their final consensus that Kazakhstan should host the Summit of the organization in 2010.

A sharp observation on this unilateral bitterness was made by Kassym-Jomart Tokayev. The former Foreign Minister, now Under Secretary General of the United Nations in Geneva, who is normally the most diplomatic of commentators told this author:

'I must openly say that President Karimov of Uzbekistan is often a thoroughly nasty person and a most unreliable neighbour. Much of his behaviour is driven by jealousy he feels towards President Nazarbayev, who always treats Karimov with respect because he is the older man by three years. But this age difference does not hide the difference between the economic and political instability of Karimov's Uzbekistan and the opposite conditions of success and stability which exist in Kazakhstan'.

The political instability is sometimes exported. Islamist extremist groups from Uzbekistan are attempting to infiltrate the schools and mosques of neighbouring states. Refugees from Karimov's repressions, notably the 2005 quelling of civil unrest which resulted in several hundred deaths, fled to Kazakhstan. Astana and Almaty are host cities to many thousands of Uzbek legal guest workers and illegal immigrants. So the tensions continue.

Despite such difficulties, trade is increasing. Uzbeks are hardworking people with particular skills in growing vegetables, cotton and other agricultural produce, although sometimes with the help of child and slave labour. As a result of such exports and its imports of oil and minerals, Uzbekistan is now within Kazakhstan's top 7 trading partners.

Looking ahead to the longer term it should be noted that Uzbekistan has an educated and youthful population, thirty-four per cent of whom are under fourteen. They are restive and discontented with Islam Karimov's regime. This seventy-five year old dictator is unpopular, but until his rule comes to an end, Uzbekistan will remain a source of trouble for Kazakhstan and the region.

Trouble has already exploded openly in Kyrgyzstan. In June 2010 serious ethnic rioting between Uzbek and Kyrgyz groups in the south of the country resulted in unprecedented violence and hundreds of dead on both sides. Since then, the country's political situation has remained as worrying as a grumbling appendix with sporadic outbreaks of violence and continuous instability even after the democratic election of a new President Roza Otunbayeva.

Despite its chaotic politics and extreme poverty, this small nation of five million people is of some strategic importance to both East and West. Kyrgyzstan is the only county in the world to be the location of large military bases for both Russia and the United States. Washington pays an annual rent of $60 million for its Manas air base which it uses as a major re-supply facility for its troops in Afghanistan. This rental is probably Kyrgyzstan's largest source of foreign currency for the country has few natural resources or exports

The Kyrgyz and the Kazakhs are kindred spirits. Their language and their culture is closely connected. Their character is similar too, although Kazakhs often use the word 'stubborn' to describe their poorer cousins. But what makes Kyrgyzstan a volatile state is neither its poverty nor its stubbornness. The volatility comes from the destabilizing rebelliousness of various groups and gangs, many of them drawn from Uzbek tribes who make up some fifteen per cent of the population.

Tradition and tribalism are still key features of life in Central Asia, nowhere more strongly than in the most backward of Kazakhstan's bordering neighbours – Turkmenistan. This is a potentially rich country, larger than California, owning the world's fourth largest natural gas reserves after Russia, Iran and Qatar. Its five million people, eighty-six per cent of whom are Turkmen, comprise the most ethnically homogeneous nation of Central Asia. Yet it is also the regions most inward looking and closed community. Few outsiders understand its governance, its economic priorities or its policies towards the outside world. For all their riches in natural resources, most Turkmens are abysmally poor. It is a country of splendid palaces but social squalor. How it spends the large revenues it receives from its annual exports of seventy billion cubic metres of natural gas is a mystery, particularly as most of the country's medical and welfare facilities were closed down by the long-serving and eccentric former President Saparmurat Niyazov who died in 2006. His successor, Kurbanguly Berdimukhamedov, has opened up new gas pipeline routes to China and Iran. But in all other respects he runs the same kind of totalitarian regime as his predecessor. Among its many restrictions, the state keeps absolute control of the media, internet access and all other freedoms. One explanation for such repression is that Turkmenistan has a western border with Afghanistan and is thought to be influenced by the Islamist extremism of the Taliban.

Set in its regional context, Kazakhstan is a far more stable and successful society than any of its neighbours. Why should this be so? The answer, in two words, is oil and leadership. President Nazarbayev has listened more carefully and governed more sensitively than any other head of state in this part of the world. He has spent his country's oil revenue wisely, even if some of his inner circle have become foolishly rich as a result. He retains the autocratic tendencies that prevail among most Asian leaders. Yet he keeps his eyes and ears open in his search for the solutions that are most workable and acceptable for his country. The surprising result of this searching is that a mixture of Central Asian traditions and European standards has delivered for Kazakhstan the most prosperous and progressive society to emerge from the post Soviet world. Its governance may not live up to all of the liberal ideals which some Western commentators believe should be universally applicable. But compared to the Bear, the Dragon and their more backward smaller neighbours the *Samruk* or golden bird of Kazakhstan is flying high. It has also been stretching its wings in some unprecedented directions for a Central Asian state – towards Europe, the United States and above all to the Presidency of the OSCE.

9

Diplomacy and the OSCE

(I) FROM MADNESS TO SUCCESS

When I first announced in public that I was going to try to get Kazakhstan made President of the OSCE everyone thought I was crazy. It was the same reaction as I had in 1994 when I announced that our new national capital would be located in Astana. Most people, including our foreign policy experts, said 'He's mad'.

Nursultan Nazarbayev[4]

President Nazarbayev's aspiration that his country should chair the Organization for Security and Cooperation in Europe was met with international hostility as well as domestic incredulity. Although the OSCE consisted of fifty-six nations, the decision making process of this international body was dominated by the US State Department. Its officials took a cautious, if not condescending, view towards OSCE members who had emerged as nation states from the break-up of the Soviet Union. This attitude was tinged with traces of cold war mentality that lingered on into the twenty-first century with new labels such as 'Moscow dominated' and 'Russian orientated'. These tended to be sweepingly applied to all capitals east of Vienna. So when Kazakhstan in 2006 declared its bid for the OSCE presidency in 2009, the initial reaction among the US foreign policy establishment was to reject it.

The counts against Kazakhstan were that it was a former Soviet Republic, an ally of Russia, a pre-dominantly Muslim country, geographically located in Asia and with an imperfect record of democracy and human rights. All these were true but stereotypes abounded in the characterization of them. The result was that the United States, supported by its closest allies including Britain, opposed and obstructed Kazakhstan's effort to chair the OSCE. The account of how the American led obstruction was overcome is a revealing and at times amusing saga of political will and personal diplomacy. A more enduring result is the impact made by Kazakhstan on the OSCE, for its 2010 presidency brought new vitality and relevance into an organization that had become moribund. Both these successes were full of surprises.

*   *   *

(II) NEUTRALIZING THE OPPOSITION

The OSCE was a child of the cold war. When the Soviet leader Leonid Brezhnev signed the Helsinki Agreement in 1975 setting up first a conference and then an organization to improve East-West relations, the initiative was hailed as a major breakthrough. The Paris charter that followed in 1990 highlighted three areas or 'baskets' of co-operation: Security and Military issues; Environmental and Economic issues and Human Dimension issues. The latter predominantly meant progress towards democracy and human rights.

At the time when Kazakhstan became an independent nation in 1991 fewer than one in a hundred thousand of its citizens had heard of the OSCE. Even the handful of politicians and diplomats who gradually grew acquainted with the organization through visits by its officials were baffled by its relevance to the crises the young country had to confront. The OSCE's apparent irrelevance was a source of particular frustration to President Nazarbayev. As he put it:

'In this part of the world in the early 1990s, people were starving. There was no food, no heat, no currency, huge economic instability and terrorism problems from the Taliban on our borders. Then along would come OSCE representatives talking about democracy. I did my best to convince them that their priorities were wrong. I would say to them 'Look, we can't develop democracy in these conditions. We need trade, business, and economic progress first.'

The dislocation between the OSCE's and Kazakhstan's priorities grew worse. Nazarbayev felt aggrieved that when his country had to cope with the disaster of the Aral Sea drying up, no help was forthcoming from the environmental side of the organization. When there were serious terrorist threats from across the border in Tajikistan, the security experts of the OSCE offered no help. But when Kazakhstan held elections in 1999, 2005 and 2007 'the OSCE people arrived in large numbers to criticise us' complained Nazarbayev.

In fact more than 1,000 OSCE and other foreign observers who monitored the parliamentary elections of 2007 did give Kazakhstan some credit for its electoral process. The OSCE observers' official report praised the 'noticeable improvement over previous elections', the calm atmosphere at the polls, the increased level of media access for opposition parties and the transparency of the Central Election Commission as the supervisory body. On the other hand OSCE observers assessed the vote count at forty per cent of the polling stations as 'bad' or 'very bad'. This judgement took the shine off the claimed eighty-eight per cent figure of support for the President's Nur Otan Party. 'Dubious at best' was one comment on the election from a senior State Department official, while the US Ambassador to the OSCE in Vienna, Julie Finley, filed a succession of 'Statements of Concern' and 'Statements of Protest' about alleged violations of human rights, media freedoms and democratic processes in Kazakhstan. These moves were seen in Astana as part of a concerted campaign by the US to oppose the country's application to become president of the organization in 2009.

Meanwhile Nazarbayev was running a campaign of his own. He produced a collective letter of support from Russia and the former Soviet republics. He embarked on an energetic lobbying drive for Kazakhstan's bid in Western European capitals, personally persuading Germany's Angela Merkel, France's Nicholas Sarkozy and Italy's Silvio Berlusconi to pledge their backing for his country's application. Nazarbayev's arguments were that the world was changing in the twenty-first century and it was time to trust an Eastern and Asian nation with the presidency. He also pointed out that American dominance had led to paralysis. The organization had not held a summit for eleven years, no US Secretary of State had attended a meeting of it for six years and the agenda had been tilted heavily towards human rights issues while ignoring the economic, security and environmental concerns that were fundamental to the original OSCE charter.

Because many member states of the OSCE were won round by Nazarbayev's lobbying, Washington had to alter its tactics. Kazakhstan's application for the presidency had at first been treated by the State Department as a joke, then as a nuisance and finally as a problem. The problem came to a head because in early fall of 2006 Nazarbayev was due to visit Washington with a schedule whose centrepiece was a meeting in the Oval office with President George W Bush.

* * *

(III) COMEDY AND CO-OPERATION AT THE WHITE HOUSE

In the days before this meeting of the two Presidents, the State Department put heavy diplomatic pressure on Kazakhstan. Secretary of State Condoleezza Rice called in the Kazakh Ambassador to Washington, Kanat Saudabayev, to advise him that Nazarbayev should not raise the OSCE chairmanship with Bush. She said it would be embarrassing to do this because the United States was maintaining its opposition to the Kazakh bid. 'Please Mr Ambassador ask your President not to make an issue of the OSCE Presidency when he comes to the White House' said Condoleezza Rice to Kanat Saudabayev.

When Nazarbayev arrived in Washington, the Kazakh Ambassador duly relayed this message adding his own advice that it would be counter-productive to ask the President of the United States for his support. This same view was taken by the Kazakh Foreign Minister, Kassym-Jomart Tokayev. Nazarbayev listened attentively to his advisers and seemed to agree with them.

When the two Presidents met, Nazarbayev initially kept silent about the OSCE as economic and foreign policy issues were discussed. But he changed his mind when his host began laying on the flattery with a trowel. As the heads of state sat by the fire in the Oval Office, George W. Bush pointed to the portrait of George Washington above the mantelpiece and said to his visitor:

'You are to Kazakhstan what George Washington is to the United States.'

'Well thank you for warm words' responded Nazarbayev. 'But if you think so highly of us how come are you so against Kazakhstan having the presidency of the OSCE?'

As Condoleezza Rice gave Ambassador Kanat Saudabayev a sharp look, the Kazakh leader pressed his point.

'You have just said we are strategic partners. Our countries are friends. I have good relations with your father. I just came here for staying the weekend with him at Kennebunkport. So I don't understand why you are so against our chairmanship.'

The President of the United States looked puzzled. 'What is the name of this organization you want to chair?' he asked.

'OSCE' replied Nazarbayev. Bush turned to his Secretary of State and asked: 'Condi, are we still members of this organization?'

The embarrassment now shifted to the American side of the discussion as the 43rd President had to be brought up to speed on the OSCE. Eventually a prompted George W. Bush tried a new tactic: 'Are you sure you really want this chairmanship?' he asked, 'Just think about it, the OSCE is an organization discussing, condemning or accusing someone on a daily basis. It won't bring you any good. They will put you under the microscope, finding faults with you, examining your accomplishments and your drawbacks and comparing Kazakhstan with other countries particularly on human rights. So think once again whether you really need this organization'[5].

Nazarbayev had thought more about it than his host. He marshalled the arguments in favour of his country taking the presidency of the organization in 2009, listing the names of the nations that supported him and concluding: 'Mr President, fifty member states of the OSCE agree with Kazakhstan's chairmanship of the OSCE but the United States does not. How can we call each other strategic partners if you continue to oppose us?' President Bush gave ground gracefully, saying to Condoleezza Rice and the other officials present: 'I think we will have to reconsider this issue'.

After such a concession it should have been game set and match to Nazarbayev. But the State Department did not give up easily. On the same evening as the Oval Office meeting, a reception was held in the White House in honour of the visiting Kazakh President. Nazarbayev was enjoying the party with a glass of wine in his hand when Condoleezza Rice approached him to say: 'Could you please reflect further on this issue? We will put you in the line for the OSCE

Presidency and do our best to deliver it to you in 2015 or 2016. By that time you will have developed your human and democratic rights.'

'No!' replied Nazarbayev. 'Let me remind you that the OSCE operates on the basis of consensus. If you block us then I assure you that Kazakhstan and Russia will block any candidate supported by the United States for the OSCE chairmanship. That is my last word to you!'

Condoleezza Rice left the reception and must have had a few last words of her own to the State Department. For within fifteen minutes she was back at the party with a new proposal for the Kazakh leader.

'We have already promised the position in 2009 to Greece', she explained, 'but would you accept the presidency of the OSCE in 2010?'

'If you are prepared to compromise then we will compromise', said Nazarbayev.

And that was how Kazakhstan won its battle to become OSCE President[6].

*   *   *

(IV) DIPLOMATIC PROGRESS ON A DIFFICULT ROAD

Even after Nazarbayev had achieved his victory, the road to the OSCE summit was not a smooth one. The main difficulty was that the organization was more dead than alive. Russia and the United States had for several years been at loggerheads about its purposes and activities. Bilateral suspicions in both Washington and Moscow had lead to international stagnation. Despite employing a staff of over 3,500, the OSCE appeared to have achieved little and forgotten nothing since its first beginnings in the cold war era.

Kazakhstan broke this impasse by a combination of diplomatic professionalizm and political leadership. The best brains in its Ministry of Foreign Affairs prepared new initiatives for the organization. At a Madrid meeting of the OSCE's Ministerial council in 2007, Kazakhstan offered a number of improvements to its own human rights record by saying it would improve some media freedoms, establish the office of an ombudsman, legitimize opposition parties, enhance human rights and make progress towards democratization. It remains a matter for argument as to how many of these 'Madrid commitments' were partially or completely fulfilled. Yet the fact that they were made in the first place enabled the entire agenda of the OSCE to move into new territory. In particular a fresh focus was given to the security challenges of the Central Asia region, to the reconstruction of Afghanistan and to resolving protracted conflicts, most notably in Nagorno-Karabakh, Moldova and Georgia.

As these moves gathered momentum, some of Kazakhstan's most vociferous critics in the US changed their tune. One prominent foe-turned-friend was Julie Finley, a former US Ambassador to the OSCE in Vienna. Speaking at a conference at the Center for Strategic and International Studies in Washington DC in July 2010 Ambassador Finley said 'In grading Kazakhstan's chairmanship of the OSCE, I give them a solid B plus. That is a big jump for me. I opposed their selection.' Ambassador Finley also praised the diplomatic team at the head of Kazakhstan's Ministry of Foreign Affairs for their implementation of the OSCE Presidency. 'They have been very open and outgoing in their leadership' she said. 'They have been centred on what is going on in Kyrgyzstan. They have been very solid and professional from the get-go. Kazakhstan has knocked my socks off.'[7]

The knocker-off-in-chief of socks within the western community of diplomats was Kanat Saudabayev. Nicknamed 'the bulldog' by his fellow Kazakh politicians, Saudabayev is an exuberant and doggedly tenacious aide-for-all-seasons to Nazarbayev. Their close links go back four decades to the Brezhnev era when they were both young provincial ministers in the Soviet Republic of Kazakhstan. Astana insiders say that 'when the President wants to get a difficult job done he appoints Saudabayev who is utterly loyal and usually delivers'.

Although Kanat Saudabayev lived up to his reputation as a pugnacious Foreign Minister and chairperson-in-office of the OSCE, the heavy lifting of delivering the agenda Kazakhstan wanted was done by its President. On the day his country assumed the chair of the organization, 14 January 2010, Nazarbayev took the unprecedented step of intervening by video in the Vienna conference at which the presidency was formally transferred. In a major speech to the assembled delegates he defined the motto of the new chairmanship as 'the four Ts – trust, transparency, tradition and tolerance'. The most important demand in his video address was that an OSCE summit should be held, to be attended by the heads of state and government of all member states. Amazingly, no such meeting had been convened for over ten years. Even so, Nazarbayev's proposal was received less than enthusiastically by some of the most important participants.

'The Americans and others kept asking me: Why? What do you need a summit for?' recalled the Kazakh leader. 'Then they objected to my invitation to hold it in Astana.'

The objections did not succeed for long. As the bulldog and his boss kept up the pressure, country after country found themselves caught out in a diplomatic game which could well have been called pass-the-summit-parcel.

'I love you, Nursultan, but if we must have a summit maybe we can hold it somewhere else, somewhere in Europe' said the French President, Nicolas Sarkozy. 'For me it is unimportant *where* the summit takes place' replied Nazarbayev. 'But it is really important that it does take place during the year of our presidency. So if you want it in Europe, let's have it in Paris.'

'Oh please no, not in Paris' responded Sarkozy.

'Well then let's hold it in Vienna. That's the home of the OSCE' said Nazarbayev[8].

The Austrians declined the honour but suggested Helsinki. 'No thank you' said the Government of Finland. After one or two further abortive offers, the game of passing the parcel was becoming exhausting. So Astana won. The last member state to sign up to an OSCE summit in Kazakhstan was the United States.

* * *

(V) COPING WITH THE CRITICS

Nazarbayev's reasons for fighting so hard for both the Presidency and the summit of the OSCE did not appeal to his critics. They accused him of grandstanding in his quest to gain greater international acceptance for Kazakhstan. Even if this was a correct assessment, it does not seem to be an unworthy motive for the head of state of a country which was then less than twenty years old. For most OSCE members would surely not begrudge a host nation's right to benefit from the limelight of an international summit. Nor should there be any complaint about Kazakhstan proclaiming the considerable economic and social achievements it has made since it emerged from the break-up of the Soviet Union. Yet there exists a vociferous international lobby of opponents who appear to be determined to deny the government in Astana any credit for its post-communist progress.

One leading platform for these critics is the London Foreign Policy Centre which in 2010 held three meetings in committee rooms at the House of Commons. The speakers at these events were mainly opposition politicians from Kazakhstan or spokesmen from human rights organizations. A leading voice and financial supporter at the meeting was Mukhtar Ablyazov who was at the time fighting a number of charges in the UK courts.

The Kazakh ambassador to Britain, Kairat Abusseitov, said politely at the end of the third of these sessions 'Thank you for your non-stop attention to my country'. Perhaps he was being ironic for the most non-stop characteristic of the meetings was attacking the ambassador about individual cases in which there had allegedly been inadequate standards of press freedom or human rights.

What was wrong about the tone and content of the Foreign Policy Centre's intense focus on Kazakhstan was not the highlighting of imperfections in the country's record of democratic and human rights. It was the absence of any recognition that there might have been the slightest of improvements in these areas since Soviet times.

There is an interesting debate to be had on the question of whether

Kazakhstan's record on issues relating to the human dimension of the OSCE can be seen as a glass half full or a glass half empty. The hostility of many human rights organizations suggest the latter, yet there has undoubtedly been progress in the fields of criminal justice reform, ethnic tolerance and religious freedom. The dialogue with the OSCE has also resulted in Kazakhstan sustaining the Office for Democratic Institutions and Human Rights (ODIHR), developing an Ombudsman's office and allowing some relaxations in the rules governing the setting up of opposition parties and freedom of the press. These changes, although regarded as too slow and too small by some critics, were unthinkable in Soviet times and are still largely unthinkable in most of the other neighbouring 'stans' or states on Kazakhstan's borders.

These and other examples suggest that the glass half full side of the human rights debate is a more sustainable case than could be imagined from listening to the loudest voices in the international human rights community. Moreover, compared to the stagnation and immobility of the OSCE itself in recent years, Kazakhstan has made some forward movements, even in the human dimension areas where it has been most sharply criticized. As for the critics themselves, they and their NGOs were all invited to the summit.

* * *

(VI) HIGH DRAMA AT THE SUMMIT

Astana played host to the first OSCE summit of the twenty-first century on 1 December 2010. The turnout of leaders from the organization's fifty-six member states was impressive. They included the US Secretary of State, Hillary Clinton, President Dimitri Medvedev of Russia, Chancellor Angela Merkel of Germany, President Nicolas Sarkozy of France, Prime Minister Silvio Berlusconi of Italy, Deputy Prime Minister Nicholas Clegg of the United Kingdom and the Presidents or Prime Ministers of Armenia, Austria, Azerbaijan, Belgium, Bulgaria,

Croatia, Finland, Greece, Hungary, Kyrgyzstan, Lithuania, Netherlands, Romania, Serbia, Switzerland, Turkey, Ukraine and many others.

For all the superficial good will among this stellar cast list, it soon became clear that their national delegations were deeply divided. 'You will have to rename this the Organization for Squabbling, Complaining and Exaggerating', grumbled one veteran US diplomat. Nazarbayev was appalled by the entrenched attitudes that surfaced. 'You soon vividly saw how polarized the situation was', he recalled, 'I had the feeling that some people were doing their best to make the summit fail'.

The Kazakhstan presidency had been hoping to reach agreement on establishing a mechanizm for resolving conflicts among member states. This proved impossible. Some of the most difficult conflicts almost seemed to worsen during the summit. The Americans and Russians resolved to score acrimonious points against each other over Georgia. The President of Armenia and Azerbaijan had a bitter row in public about their Nagorno-Karabakh dispute. When it came to announcing the final declaration there was an impasse. The scheduled one hour break for drafting the document expanded into a six hour stand-off. Nazarbayev was reduced to taking his most prominent guests on a personally conducted tour of Astana. When he returned from this diversion the OSCE secretariat reported that there was not enough common ground for an agreed final declaration. Instead there would have to be a heavily diluted protocol merely re-stating the aims of the organization. This meant the summit would end 'not with a bang but a whimper'.

President Nazarbayev refused to accept this failure. He cajoled many reluctant member states into signing up. This was a particularly difficult task because some of the key players had already flown home. 'I was not going to be beaten', Nazarbayev recalled, 'So I went back to my house that night and called one by one those Presidents who had departed and asked them to instruct their representatives to support the final declaration which they had already agreed in principle. After about four hours on the telephone I was successful. The last one I persuaded to sign was the President of Armenia'.

This brinkmanship achieved the required breakthrough. At 1 a.m. on the morning of 3 December Nazarbayev returned to announce the agreed declaration to the conference hall, 'I was cheered like a Hollywood celebrity', he joked. Silvio Berlusconi behaved as though he was presenting his host with a Hollywood Oscar. 'We love you Mr President! We love you! You are a great man!' was the Italian leader's effusive benediction.

As the nocturnal dust settled, some commentators saw the outcome more positively. 'It's the most important summit we've had in twenty-five years since Ronald Reagan and Mikhail Gorbachev broke the ice between them in Reykjavik in 1986', said UPI editor Martin Smith on *Fox News*.

Other pundits also looked beyond the chaos of the divergent conference speeches. They hailed one or two significant side results such as the decision by Belarus, the former Soviet Republic, to give up its weapon grade uranium and to sign the nuclear non-proliferation accords. Above all the media coverage respected the achievement of holding the first OSCE summit for eleven years. The fact that the organization will continue to hold top level meetings suggested that the OSCE is coming out of its coma and that its diplomatic machinery may soon achieve more than looked possible in the hours before Nazarbayev broke the diplomatic log jam.

This was certainly the view taken by the OSCE's General Secretary Marc Perrin de Brichambaut. He claimed that 'ninety per cent agreement' had been achieved by the proposed, but shelved, action plan on resolving conflicts and that a final version of it would be implemented during the coming year. 'So please do not describe the outcome of the summit as a failure.'[9]

Even though the diplomatic results of the summit were cloudy, the domestic responses to it were enthusiastic. For after making allowances for the over-jubilant tone of the state television reporting, it was clear that the people of Kazakhstan at all levels took great pride in what they saw as a landmark national event. From lowly waiters and labourers to the high intelligentsia just about everyone talked up the OSCE gathering of fifty-six Presidents, Prime Ministers and Foreign Ministers as the most important symbol of international recognition that the country had ever received. Even Nazarbayev's internal critics on the international human rights scene acknowledged that they and their in-country NGOs had been impeccably hosted and heard. They may have advanced their own agenda better than they recognized. As the OSCE's General Secretary put it, 'The forces working to develop civil society in Kazakhstan will have been greatly encouraged by this process ... thanks to the OSCE the country's younger generation has witnessed debates about democracy and progress that may have laid the ground for future reforms'[10].

Whatever the long term future consequences of the OSCE's 2010 summit in Astana, the short term outcome enhanced Kazakhstan's international standing. 'Suddenly there is praise for Kazakh diplomats blessed with decent event management skills and eager to enhance their country's standing' reported *The Economist*[11], 'the talk now is of an OSCE that has been re-invigorated after losing its direction in the past decade'.

Re-invigoration, recognition and respect are creditable results. When it is recalled that Nazarbayev's first bid for the presidency of the organization was greeted with derision and opposition in key western capitals, it is no exaggeration to describe the saga of the OSCE summit the fulfilment of an impossible dream.

10

The Education Revolution

(I) A SYSTEM THAT NEEDED TO CHANGE

Education has been a problem but is becoming an opportunity in post independence Kazakhstan. Until recently this was a sector of the nation's life that lagged behind the progress of all other development. Although the government produced superficially impressive statistics about the tenfold increase in its educational spending and the numbers of its newly built schools (750), nursery schools (1,117) or pre-school facilities (5,302), behind the figures lay a multitude of failures.

Apart from an imaginative programme called *Bolashak* ('the future') which each year sends 3,000 young scholarship winners overseas to study for their degrees at international universities (see pp. 177–80), the reality is that much of Kazakhstan's education system lost its way during the first seventeen years or so after the collapse of the Soviet Union. Having rejected the Soviet educational model, which in its monolithic way had many good qualities, the Kazakhs tried to invent their own schools and their own curriculum but ended up with widespread mediocrity. With one or two exceptions, notably Almaty's western-style KIMEP University, the higher education sector fared little better.

But by 2009, as the country emerged from the worldwide banking crisis and recession, a flurry of Presidential decrees and ministerial decisions changed the policies and priorities of schools and universities. As Kazakhstan reaches the anniversary marking its first twenty years of independence, a new momentum and sense of direction has swept through its educational system. There is now a better funded and more energized spirit of transformation in the country's schools and universities, as I found on my travels around some of the most interesting examples of the changes in the system.

* * *

(II) THE INTELLECTUAL AND OTHER SCHOOLS

Astana's Intellectual School gave a hospitable and interesting welcome to this author. After I had toured its facilities which included computers in every classroom, state of the art science labs and a surprising number of outsize chess sets in the common rooms, the fifth and sixth forms put on a cultural presentation. It consisted of traditional folk dancing, a dombra concert, a violin solo and speeches of welcome by the head boy and head girl.

Then it was my turn to go up to the podium to respond to the students questions. This question and answer session ranged far and wide. Who were my favourite authors and why? Who were the most inspirational leaders I had met in my career and why? How did the British Parliament make its laws? What was the EU's attitude to the OSCE? Was the International Baccalaureate recognized by all universities in the UK and Europe? What were my working methods as an author? What was my advice to young writers who want to get their books published?

I was then invited to ask the pupils questions. How many of them expected to go to university? (All). How had they been selected for their places at the school? (A competitive exam process). In a syllabus that specializes in mathematics and science does your school give enough attention to history and the arts? (We need to have more classes in these subjects). What impact does Chinese literature and culture have on your curriculum? (Some). What are your favourite authors? (Tolstoy and Abay). Where do you hope to find jobs? (The oil industry and the government were first and second choices).

The session was lively with a fair amount of laughter and some engaging disagreements among the teenagers. It did not appear to be a stilted or rehearsed event. Having made well over fifty school visits during my career as a politician I thought this one was among the best. This was because of a great surprise. The schools fifth and sixth formers conducted the entire dialogue with me in fluent English – even though we were in the heart of Kazakhstan's capital.

The obviously successful school I visited is one of twenty-six in a new educational initiative known as The Intellectual Schools. They needed to be created because in the years after independence Kazakhstan's school system crumbled into second rate standards. President Nazarbayev, who was himself the beneficiary of many first rate teachers in the village schools he attended during the Soviet era of the 1950s, came to a belated recognition of the country's educational weakness. 'Our schools, especially in rural areas, had low standards and were in poor condition. But there is still time to improve them' he says 'We have too many old buildings made out of wood and mud bricks. We do not have sufficient teachers. We did build 750 secondary schools but that is not nearly enough. So we have an overloaded system which in some parts of the country has to take three shifts of school children each day. We should have done more to improve things, but now we are reforming the whole system'.[13]

The Intellectual Schools are spearheading the reform program. Twenty-six of them have been or are in the process of being commissioned. Their funding is three times greater than the expenditure on an average school and the capital for their new buildings and class room facilities, comes out of a separate budget. Most of the extra money goes on the teachers salaries, which are as low as $200 a month in ordinary schools, a figure which sometimes gives rise to petty corruption for rigged exam results. No such temptation should occur among the elite teachers selected for the new Intellectual Schools. They are paid salaries between five and seven times higher than the norm. At the Intellectual School in Astana which I visited the lowest paid teacher was receiving $650 a month and the highest remuneration for heads of department was $1,500 a month. In addition all these teachers received free housing and other benefits such as annual $500 a year allowance to buy the latest books on their subject. 'Our salaries are now so attractive that we are getting applications from university professors to teach here' said the school's chairperson Mrs Kulyash Shamshiddinova 'but we want to recruit the best because our pupils are among the most gifted children in the country'[14]

This elitist approach, revolutionary in its concept for a former communist country, is fostered by each Intellectual School being run by a Joint Stock Company. This is a non-profit corporation with local and national tiers of management whose senior board of directors includes prominent figures such as the Deputy Prime Minister and the Minister of Education. Hovering over them is the prominent figure of President Nazarbayev who takes an immense personal interest in these schools. They carry his name as Nazarbayev Intellectual Schools and a large part of their budgets come from the Nazarbayev Fund which is a pocket of national expenditure designated for special educational initiatives.

The Intellectual Schools are founded on two visions. The first is to establish an initial twenty-six centres of academic excellence teaching their pupils in three languages, Kazakh, Russian and English. Some of the schools will offer courses in additional foreign languages notably Chinese, German, French and (in Semipalatinsk) Japanese. There is particular emphasis on mathematics and science in the curriculum. All grades in the final certificate of Secondary Education are awarded in International Baccalaureate or in other internationally recognized examinations such as IELT, TOEFL or SATS I and II. The 6,000 or so pupils who are educated at these flagship Intellectual Schools will form an intellectual elite of the nation's best and brightest brains. As Nazarbayev put it in the speech he made in Almaty launching the program entitled 'Intellectual Breakthrough to the Future': 'It is necessary to create the core of the national intellect, to establish schools which will became a foundation of Kazakhstan's brainpower.'

The second part of the vision is to grow these flagship Intellectual Schools into a much larger fleet of higher quality schools throughout the country. This will be a challenging task for there are over 7,500 secondary schools in Kazakhstan, fifty-two per cent of them in poor rural areas. There is great pressure on the government to deliver higher educational standards. 'Schooling is the hottest topic in the country right now' says the Minister of Education Bakhytzan Zhumagulov 'so we are having to catch up fast to meet the demand. The enrolment of schoolchildren is soaring and as a government we are now spending six per cent of GDP on education.'

In addition to the rise of the public expenditure, the private funding of primary, secondary and higher education is a strong feature of Kazakh life. There is an old saying 'every villager will sell his last cow to give his son a good education.' It is an attitude which produces financial support from parents to many schoolchildren whether they are being taught in crumbling shacks in deprived parts of the countryside or at the new showpiece Intellectual Schools in prosperous city centres. This support is usually just a small percentage contribution to the total costs of educating a pupil but it makes the engagement of parents in their child's schooling an important force for improvement.

*   *   *

(III) HAILEYBURY

As in many Western societies, a minority of families can afford to send their children to private fee-paying schools. They are one hundred and fourteen of them of which the most expensive is Haileybury College Almaty. This is an offshoot of its namesake, a famous independent school in Haileybury, England.

The founder and chairman of the governors of Haileybury College Almaty – Central Asia's first school to be created on the traditional British model – is Serzhan Zhumashev. He is a multi-millionaire Kazakh real estate developer whose projects have ranged from five star hotels in Moscow to skyscrapers in his native Almaty. Zhumashev, who sent his son to be educated at Haileybury England, conceived the idea of creating a franchised and identically named school in Kazakhstan.

The Haileybury brand has transplanted well. Three years after its initial opening the school, which cost $50 million tobuild, now has 450 pupils whose parents pay fees that range from between $5,000 and $9,000 a term, depending on the age of the student. Architecturally the Almaty version of Haileybury is a modernist gem with high airy ceilings, a spectacular atrium, a spacious library and huge expanses of windows looking out to the beautiful Alatau mountains which tower over the classrooms and playing fields.

The founding headmaster of Haileybury College Almaty is Andrew Auster. He came from Orwell Park School in England which he had led for thirteen successful years. He has found it easy to recruit a good teaching staff of eighty (over half of them UK expatriates) since the school can offer pensionable tax free salaries of up to $40,000 a year.

Academically the school provides a quintessentially English education. It teaches in the English language (but with some classes in Kazakh) and its curriculum could only have been devised by the truest of true and traditional Brits. On my visit in early 2011 the notice boards were announcing special projects to commemorate the four hundredth anniversary of the King James Bible and a study of the career of Prime Minister Clement Attlee (an old Haileyburian). These subjects seemed somewhat rarefied for young Kazakhstani children to be studying but this anglicized imprimatur is stamped on everything Haileybury stands for, from Oxford and Cambridge Examination Board A Levels to school uniforms from Harrods.

'We have taken great trouble to develop the right ethos for the school' says Andrew Auster. 'The Kazakh parents here are looking for a broad liberal education to civilize and change their children into innovative, articulate and competitive young people.'

The verb 'civilize' was an appropriate term for the Headmaster to use, for when the school opened its doors with three hundred and sixty new boys and girls in September 2008 some of them were so spoilt and savage that they seemed hostile to the whole process of learning. 'We had quite a few troublemakers who wanted to slop around in jeans, play their I-pods, bring their own butlers and not do any work at all', says Andrew Aster, 'but we imposed the necessary discipline even though we had to ask some boys to leave. And now we have a successful and growing school which has just passed its first OFSTED inspection with flying colours'.

Hailebury's colours are flying so high that a second franchised school with the same name has just been opened in the national capital with a construction and endowment price tag close to $100 million.

The founding patron of Haileybury Astana is Bolat Utemuratov, an important Kazakh financier whose career has taken him from local butcher to international banker. Andrew Auster has transferred as

Headmaster to the new school which admitted its first pupils a few weeks before the country's independence celebrations in 2011. Six months ahead of its official opening, the plans and schedules for Haileybury Astana seemed to be in some disarray. But it is often the Kazakhstanis' way that projects come together at the eleventh hour, so in the end the new school started on schedule. Although the two Haileyburys are likely to be the flagships for independent education in the country for some time, several other smaller competitors have started up so the sector is vibrant and expanding.

In addition to the independent schools, there are a growing number of Islamic schools or *madressas*. In a 2009 interview this development was concerning President Nazarbayev for he said to this author:

'It has become a fashionable trend among businessmen over recent years to erect *madressas* in their villages. The problem is that once they are built it is often not clear who should be teaching our young people here or what syllabus they should be following. We need a law to straighten out these issues.'[14]

Although no law covering *madressas* has yet been enacted, the Ministry of Education, which licenses all schools, has highlighted its inspection regime and now says that the questions being asked about Islamic teaching are 'a manageable problem'. Some observers disagree and feel that Islamic schools financed by Wahhabi and other fundamentalist sects are a growing worry.

The Ministry of Education has many higher priorities on its agenda. One is the surge in demand for pre-school places, a sector which deteriorated sharply because of the collapse of the Soviet Union brought with it the collapse of the kindergarten system. Today Kazakhstan has over a million children under the primary school starting age of seven but less than a third of them receive any sort of early years education. This is a gap which the government is struggling to close with its *Balapan* or 'little chick' program. It includes an accelerated kindergarten school building initiative; the streamlining of pre-schools licensing and significant government subsidies paid to private pre-schools for each pupil they enrol. 'This is one of our biggest challenges' says Education Vice Minister Mahmetgali Sarybekov 'we are expanding our pre-school network to serve eighty per cent of the demand within three years and we hope to provide places for one hundred per cent of our youngest children within five years.'

Another major priority is to increase the number of years children spend at school from eleven to twelve by 2015. This sounds a straightforward objective but it requires a complex restructuring of the curriculum at all levels, an expansion of classroom space and the training of teachers in the new twelfth year courses.

Inadequate teaching remains a major problem. Along with the entire post Soviet school system, Kazakhstan's 270,000 teachers became demoralized in the 1990s. Low pay was a key element in this loss of motivation for most teachers salaries fell to around sixty per cent of the national average wage. 'Unfortunately we reached the point where the social and economic standards of our classroom educators did not match the requirements of the noble pedagogic profession' says Education Minister Bakytzhan Zhumagulov. He is doing his best to reverse this trend, greatly helped by innovations such as extra finance from both public and private sources. These innovations include a per capita voucher system which transfers money with pupils to move to the more successful schools; the recruitment of foreign teachers and above all the opening of the new Intellectual Schools. They are giving the best and brightest members of the teaching profession a huge boost in terms of increased remuneration and improved recognition. But education ministers are at pains to emphasize that the rise in teaching standards is happening throughout the 7,500 schools across the country and not just in the new elite group. Teaching has been officially designated 'prestigious work' and improved pay is now following the improved prestige.

How well and how quickly these efforts to upgrade the quality of the nation's teachers will work is difficult to predict. What can be said is that Kazakhstan's schools at every level are now receiving so much political attention and financial investment that a revolution is under way in pre-school, primary and secondary education.

*   *   *

(IV) THE UNIVERSITIES

The revolution is not confined to schools. Kazakhstan's universities are also being upgraded. Some of them are being replaced or supplemented by new institutions. This process is badly needed. Until last year the country claimed to have one hundred and forty-six universities of which forty-eight were state funded and ninety-eight were private institutions. Now the number has been reduced to sixty. Yet, for a national population of sixteen million, this is still too large a number of higher education establishments. Some of them are not worthy to be called universities. The whole sector is in urgent need of rationalization, rejuvenation and the creation of new universities of real academic excellence.

The best place to see how the University revolution is taking shape is at the brand new Nazarbayev University in Astana. Its two hundred acre campus opened its doors in September 2010, admitting the first 485 students (selected from 4,000 applicants) to do a foundation course called the University Preparatory Certificate (UPC) programme. The UPC concentrates on teaching the students' academic English and other major subjects in the natural and social sciences. This foundation course will lead on to undergraduate, graduate and postgraduate programs with sixty-four per cent of the students taking their degrees or doctorates in maths and physics, sixteen per cent in chemistry and biology and twenty per cent in social sciences. 'Our vision is to create a prestigious world class university in compliance with the highest international standards' say NU's first president Dr Aslan Sarinzhipov, a former senior executive with the World Bank's education division. He is being helped in this task by a teaching staff seconded from ten renowned international institutions including University College London, Harvard School of Medicine, University of Pennsylvania, Duke University Business School, Carnegie Mellon University, University Wisconsin-Madison and the National University of Singapore.

When I visited Nazarbayev University (NU) six weeks after it opened, the newly arrived students looked rather overhoused in their $200 million worth of pristine campus buildings. Their centre piece is a spectacularly cavernous atrium whose great glass ceilings seemed vaguely reminiscent of a space age airport. But the wide open spaces at NU will soon fill up, because the student body is expected to leap from under 500 in 2010 to over 6,000 by 2020. Most of the graduates will focus their studies on applied rather than pure science with the objective that they will be qualified to fill the employment needs of Kazakhstan industries, particularly the oil and gas industry.

I met many of the first students and the first teaching staff including fifty-five lecturers and professors who had just arrived from University College London. 'Of course there are challenges in a brand new university, particularly as all the teaching here will be done in English, which is why the foundation course is so important' said Professor Chris Fenwick 'but we are not imposing our UCL programmes nor are we trying to copy any other University. This is a genuine partnership between the international partners and the Kazakh founders.'

NU's founder in chief is President Nazarbayev. Initially he did not allow the university to bear his name. But he changed his mind because of his determination to create a world class university in his country. Previous attempts to do this had failed, most notably the much touted Eurasian University in Astana. But now that Nazarbayev has given his personal imprimatur to NU, optimists hope that he will provide both the political drive and economic funding to improve the new institution's chances of international success. He is certainly in a hurry to make it succeed as he showed when he appointed NU's new head Aslan Sarinzhipov, who had been working on blueprints for the university from his position at the World Bank. As Sarinzhipov recalled: 'The President said to me:

"since you're so smart, do the job yourself and do it quickly because I am an old man now. I will guarantee to support you for three years. You have one year to get the foundation course up and running, one year for starting the undergraduate program and one year to start the graduate program".'

President Nazarbayev must surely have had his tongue in cheek when he portrayed himself as an old man in a hurry who might only have time to provide NU with financial support for its first three years. The reality is that the education revolution is a long term plan. NU will be generously funded both by the state and by the Narabayev Fund. This provides scholarships for both the Intellectual School and NU from a foundation that has been established by private contributions. Major donors include the Foundation of the First President of Kazakhstan, leading companies including the oil majors and prominent businessmen.

This mixture of private funding and state expenditure which runs all Kazakhstan's education system brings an element of competitive tension which is ultimately beneficial. This is recognized by the former NU President Aslan Sarinzhipov who says:

'We are in the market place in which we have to compete. We may have certain advantages because we expect to be able to draw on the talented students who will be coming out of the Intellectual Schools with good IB qualifications. But our biggest competition is not with other local universities but with international universities. This is because every year 30,000 Kazakhstan students go abroad for their higher education. We hope to keep many more of them staying at home to get their degrees at NU.'

Recently Mr Shigeo Katsu, the former Vice-President of the World Bank, has been named as the new President of NU and Aslan Sarinzhipov has become the CEO of the Joint Stock Company which manages NU.

Nazarbayev University does have one serious domestic competitor apart from the international institutions of higher education. This is Almaty's KIMEP – the Kazakhstan Institute of Management, Economics and Strategic Planning. It claims to be a world class university attracting over 4,400 students who take their degrees in economics, law, social sciences, international relations, public administrations and business studies.

KIMEP takes pride in being a western-style university. Its classes are taught exclusively in English. It has 270 full time members of the faculty who receive salaries ranging from $80,000 to $125,000. 170 of the faculty hold PhDs or the equivalent from Western academic institutions, most of them coming from the US, Canada and the UK.

The founder President of KIMEP is Dr Chan Young Bang. A Korean born US citizen, he taught economics at UCLA and the University of San Francisco before becoming a close adviser to President Nazarbayev in the early years of independence. Kazakhstan needed its own high quality institution of higher education so with Nazarbayev's encouragement Dr Bang created KIMEP in 1992 on the crumbling campus of a former High School run by the Central Committee of the Communist Party in Soviet times.

Today KIMEP is a modern private university, sixty per cent owned by Dr Bang's non-profit foundation and forty per cent owned by the state. There are occasional tensions in this relationship. For example KIMEP's licence was arbitrarily suspended for three months in September 2010 which cynics said was a manoeuvre by the Ministry of Education to give a boost to student enrolment at the new Nazarbayev University in Astana. But KIMEP survived the interruption and continues to receive both the full support of President Nazarbayev and a high enrolment of students whose numbers will rise to 5,600 in 2012.

KIMEP enjoys a reputation within Kazakhstan for guaranteeing its graduates a ticket to some of the best jobs offered by international companies and domestic institutions. The university runs a vigorous internship programme with private and public organizations such as Proctor and Gamble, Renault, Agip, RBS, Kaz Munai Gaz, HSBC, Kazakh Telecom, Nestlé, PriceWaterhouse Coopers, Deloitte, Air Astana and the UN.

KIMEP also has its own career and employment office which has for many years found jobs for over ninety per cent of its students at the time of their graduation. 'If you look round the biggest companies in this country they are eighty per cent staffed at management level by our graduates' says Dr Bang. 'This is the most important measurement of our success. Domestically we are making a major contribution to this country's economic future and internationally we are connected to universities all over the world whose professors come to teach here both in our regular courses and at our summer programme. Considering that the fees for our students are only $6,000 a year we offer one of the best value for money opportunities in our degree courses that you can find. Also our students are continually rising so we are increasingly respected as a world class university'.

* * *

(V) *BOLASHAK*

Although respect for KIMEP and some other home grown Kazakhstan universities is rising, their acceptance is far from complete among the coming generation of the country's students. It is an eye-opening figure that 30,000 young Kazakhs a year go overseas to international colleges and universities. Of this total, 27,000 are funded by their families or by local businesses. The remaining 3,000 are on scholarships from the state under a scheme known as the *Bolashak* program. The story of *Bolashak* is seminal to the present era of change in Kazakh education. For this scheme, launched in the difficult days of post independence economic chaos, offered the brightest young students of the country an opportunity to be educated abroad at the highest levels of academic excellence.

Bolashak (literal translation: The Future) was Nazarbayev's brain-child. The idea came to him in 1993 when he visited Singapore, as he has recalled:

'The trigger for *Bolashak* and for the educational reforms that followed it much later was Singapore. At that time I had many priorities to take care of at home, particularly finding food and jobs for people during a tough economic crisis. But as I looked at what Lee Kwan Yew's Singapore had achieved I said to myself "this is a country with no natural resources – they even have to buy their own drinking water from Malaysia. How come they have achieved all this?" It is because they have so many well educated people and a highly qualified work force. So when I came back I started to build the foundations for a highly educated group of future leaders. Even though it was the worst of times, I launched the *Bolashak* programme.'

In 1994 when the government coffers were almost empty and

desperately short of foreign currency, one hundred and eighty of Kazakhstan's cleverest students were given scholarships to overseas universities. At a cost of $10 million, the state paid every last cent of their tuition fees, travel expenses and living costs. This was the start of *Bolashak* described by Nazarbayev as 'planting our seed corn'. In the past seventeen years this scheme has sent 73,000 young Kazakhs to study for degrees at many of the world's best known higher education institutions.

Today 3,000 *Bolashak* scholarships are awarded each year to Universities such as Oxford, Cambridge, Harvard, MIT, The Sorbonne, Moscow State University and to a wide spectrum of international colleges operating in technical and scientific qualifications. The geographical spread of *Bolashak* leans towards universities in the UK which take thirty-seven per cent of the scholars and the USA taking twenty-six per cent. But another twenty-four countries welcome the elite Kazakh students including Russia (ten per cent), China, Canada, Germany, France, Malaysia, Singapore, Switzerland and Japan.

Any international visitor to the upper echelons of business and government in today's Kazakhstan soon becomes aware of *Bolashak* graduates and postgraduates. Their work ethics, ambition, attitudes and outward-looking approach are quite different to those who were raised entirely in the old Soviet shaped domestic educational system. Many of them are now rising if not risen stars in banks, big companies, government departments or entrepreneurial businesses which they themselves have started. 'We are this country's equivalent of Rhodes Scholars', said one proud Stanford graduate now a partner in an international law firm in Almaty.

This self conscious elite is developing into a powerful network within the country. Its mystique as a magic circle of tomorrow's leaders is deliberately fostered by Nazarbayev. He sees them regularly at *Bolashak* receptions, takes a well-informed interest in their progress, encourages them and often gives them fast-track promotion within this government.

A *Bolashak* scholarship, for which the competition is fierce, places every successful candidate under a contractual obligation to come back and work in Kazakhstan for a five year period after graduating abroad. Since the employment opportunities are so good, most of the scholars are happy to do this.

And for all the legends of dizzying ascents to pinnacles of power and wealth by returning *Bolashakians*, the vast majority of scholars in the programme get their jobs in more predictable areas such as engineering, medicine, mining, veterinary science, art and design. One of the many *Bolashak* students met by this author was twenty-two-year-old Danick Beshymbaev from Astana. He was half way through his four-year degree course in aerospace engineering at the Wentworth Institute of Technology in Boston.

'I get all my tuition fees and accommodation expenses paid by the programme' (he said). 'Then on top of that I am given a living expenses allowance of $1,700 a month and an air ticket back home once a year. The package costs the government around $50,000 for all my costs, so I am fantastically grateful to get this opportunity. With my aerospace engineering degree I may work for one of the air transport companies. Or I may stay on in the US and get an MBA at somewhere like MIT. Then I will try to found my own aerospace company.'

This author has met many *Bolashak* students at various stages of their careers and has yet to find a seriously discontented or disappointed one. Yet the obvious success of this international programme has created a domestic problem. Because of the gulf between *Bolashak* and the rest, every thoughtful observer of the country's development is aware that Kazakhstan has a lot of catching up to do. But the good news is that the nation's educational revolution has started. The people, particularly parents, are willing it to succeed. After the management of the economy, the management of schools and universities is Kazakhstan's greatest challenge for the twenty-first century.

11
Last Word

By the time this book is published, Kazakhstan will be celebrating the twentieth anniversary of its independence on 16 December 2011. Great festivities are planned including pageants, concerts, sports contests, historical exhibitions and firework displays on a spectacular scale rarely matched in the West.

Whatever the impact of these commemorative events, they will be outstripped by the patriotic emotions of a country coming of age with a surge of national self confidence.

International recognition is an important ingredient of this surge. The economic success story speaks for itself. But deeper still is the pride Kazakhstani people feel at being part of a nation that is playing an increasingly significant role on the world stage. The old complexes about being subjugated nomads, displaced exiles and Soviet vassals have all but disappeared. Instead, Astana now symbolizes a new mood of assertive internationalism.

Aided by its iconic architecture, Kazakhstan's capital is becoming a well recognized conference centre for global dialogues between East and West, Europe and Asia, North and South, Islam and other world religions.

Since this book went to print with its detailed account of the groundbreaking OSCE summit in December 2010 (see Chapter 9) Astana has hosted the Asian Winter Games; the World Islamic Economic Forum; the Shanghai Cooperation Council and the International Forum for a Nuclear Weapons-Free World. Such major events are accompanied by other global gatherings which make smaller headlines yet achieve bigger results. These are ministerial meetings on subjects such as anti-terrorism measures, customs regulations and healthcare. Behind them come a steady flow of cultural activities, trade negotiations and banking seminars. The world which two decades ago barely knew where Kazakhstan was, has become a world which beats many paths to the door of its capital city.

Astana is not just a well situated and well equipped location for global meetings at the crossroads of Asia and Europe. It does not play host to its diplomatic political visitors in the self-effacing style of a Geneva or Vienna. Instead it has become a venue with a vision. For President

Nazarbayev likes to influence, if not set, the agenda of the international organizations he welcomes to his capital.

Take for example his speech at the opening of the seventh World Islamic Economic Forum in June 2011. This somewhat self congratulatory and soporific body, an offshoot of the OIC (the Organisation of Islamic Conference) was startled to be lectured by Nazarbayev on its lack of success and progress. After highlighting the embarrassing fact that the Muslim world has twenty per cent of the world's population yet has not produced a single member of the G8 group of leading economies, The President of Kazakhstan demanded a series of modernization initiatives after asking the forum these questions:

'How many Islamic universities are in the world's top one hundred?
How many Nobel Prize winners in science and technology have Muslim countries produced?
How many important technological breakthroughs have come from Muslim researchers?
The answer to all: none'.

Nazarbayev's surprizing approach evidently struck a chord with his fellow Islamic leaders. For later in the same month as his Astana speech, Kazakhstan has hosted the Foreign Ministers meeting of OIC and was elected chair of the OIC Organization which changed its name to the Organisation of Islamic Cooperation.

The head of an Islamic nation who leads by implementing policies of tolerance, moderation and modernization is a surprising force to be reckoned with in the multi-polar world of the twenty-first century.

Such surprises at home and abroad are likely to be a continuing feature of Kazakhstani leadership as long as Nursultan Nazarbayev remains his country's President. As for how long will that be? Outsiders may wring their hands at the lack of any succession planning, but inside the country there is popular acceptance that Nazarbayev is going on. He has just been re-elected to a five year term, so neither he nor his people are in a hurry to create a vacancy.

When I last spoke to the President I did not ask him any questions about the succession. Instead I wondered it he would enjoy it if I ended this book, as I did my biography of him, with the Sophocles story. Nazabayev laughed and agreed.

The Sophocles story is an in-joke between biographer and subject. The circumstances were that I was conducting the last of my twenty-three hours of one-on-one interviewing with the President for my previous book *Nazarbayev and the Making of Kazakhstan*. On what I then thought was a valedictory note about the President's legacy, I quoted the words of Sophocles: 'Sometimes one has to wait until the evening to see how glorious the day has been'. To this Nazarbayev riposted 'What makes you think I have reached the evening?!'

The obvious conclusion and a good one for Kazakhstan, is that Nursultan Nazarbayev has many more years ahead of him as President of this surprising and successful country.

Endnotes

1. This 280 page report, Locked Up Potential:A Strategy for reforming prisons and rehabilitating prisoners was published by the Centre for Social Justices 2009
2. Moved to agricultural academic and science sector after 3 April 2011 presidential elections
3. New Agriculture Minister since April 2011
4. Source Note: NN interview with JA 4/11/10
5. Source Note: Tokayev, Kassym-Jomart – Meeting The Challenge (New York Global Scholarly Publications 2004)
6. Source Note: Author's interview with President Nazarbayev 1.11.2010
7. Source Note: London *Daily Telegraph* 4/9/2010
8. Source Note: Author's interview with President Nazarbayev 1/11/2010
9. Source Note: Central Asia Newswire 3/12/2010
10. Source Note: *The Economist* 4/12/2010; Central Asia Newswire 5/12/2010
11. Source Note: *The Economist* 4/12/2010
12. Source Note: Author's interview 1 November 2010
13. Source Note: Author's interview 23 October 2010
14. Source Note: Narzabayev and the Making of Kazakhstan p198

Index

191